Magistrates at work

Magistrates at work

SENTENCING AND SOCIAL STRUCTURE

Sheila Brown

OPEN UNIVERSITY PRESS
Milton Keynes · Philadelphia

Open University Press
Celtic Court
22 Ballmoor
Buckingham
MK18 1XW

and
1900 Frost Road, Suite 101
Bristol, PA 19007, USA

First Published 1991

British Library Cataloguing in Publication Data

Brown, Sheila
   Magistrates at work : sentencing and social structure.
   1. England. Young offenders. Sentencing
   I. Title
   344.20587
   ISBN 0-335-09651-4
   ISBN 0-335-09650-6 (pbk)

Library of Congress Cataloging-in-Publication Data

Brown, Sheila, 1960–
   Magistrates at work : sentencing and social structure/Sheila Brown.
      p.   cm.
   Includes bibliographical references and index.
   ISBN 0-335-09651-4 — ISBN 0-335-09650-6 (pbk.)
   1. Sentences (Criminal procedure)—Great Britain. 2. Juvenile justice,
Administration of—Great Britain.   3. Judicial process—Great Britain.   I. Title.
KD8481.B76 1991
345.41′087—dc20
[344.10587]
                                                                    90-45380
                                                                         CIP

Typeset by Inforum Typesetting, Portsmouth.
Printed in Great Britain by St Edmundsbury Press,
Bury St Edmunds, Suffolk

Contents

Preface

This book is based on a research study carried out during the period 1985–88 in six court areas in the north and north-east of England. Its major aim is to place the 'social information question' in the English juvenile court at the centre of current debates in juvenile justice. This is not a study of social work or of the impact of information on sentencing. It is a study of how magistrates perceive the social background of the defendants who appear before them in the juvenile court; of how these perceptions are produced by, and produce, the nature of sentencing in the juvenile court; and above all, of how juvenile offenders are sentenced on the basis of images of their lives which probably bear little relationship to the lived reality of those lives. The book is also, therefore, a study in the construction of knowledge in organizational life; a study in the nature of magisterial decision making; and above all, I hope, a study of the exercise of power within and beyond the boundaries of the courtroom. It attempts to show how the individual, rendered powerless during the sentencing process, is successively displaced and reconstructed as a 'case' like any other; a case which has a central significance in the social production of surveillance and control.

The book begins with a theoretical agenda, moves through to an analysis of empirical data, including interviews with over 90 magistrates, observation material from the six courts, and an analysis of social inquiry reports; and concludes by engaging with some of the current practice debates over social information in the juvenile court. Practitioners may therefore wish to avoid Chapter 1; the more theoretically inclined may wish to avoid Chapter 9. While this is possible, I hope that they will wish to return to the chapters which they have eschewed. If not, the fault is probably mine.

Acknowledgements

I would like to thank the clerks to the justices in six courts who kindly agreed to my intruding upon the difficult business of sentencing juveniles. Many thanks are also due to the 92 magistrates whose willingness to open themselves to scrutiny made this study possible, and to the court staff who patiently accommodated my needs.

There are, as always, additional debts which somehow demand to be singled out for attention. Many thanks to Pat Carlen for her advice and encouragement and to John Macmillan for his unfailing support and many invaluable discussions.

Abbreviations

AC	Attendance centre
CJA	Criminal Justice Act
DC	Detention centre
IT	Intermediate treatment
IIT	Intensive intermediate treatment
PO	Probation officer
SIR	Social inquiry report
SO	Supervision order
SSD	Social services department
TIC	(Charges) taken into account
YC	Youth custody

CHAPTER 1

Routines and relevance: the role of social information in the juvenile court

We've got to try and see why they're doing it and it nearly always comes back to home life . . . they just haven't got that kind of support, the family group is just completely disintegrating really.

> Magistrate on the relevance of social information, January 1986

Crime prevention begins in the home . . . where effective family control is lacking, children are more likely to grow up without self discipline . . they are more likely to commit crimes.

> *Crime, Justice and Protecting the Public* (Home Office), 1990

Social information – information about the family background, personal characteristics, health, social and possibly school life of offenders – is central to the day to day operation of the juvenile court. The concern voiced by the magistrate quoted above will be echoed many times by her colleagues during the course of this book as the 'magistrates' eye view' of sentencing juvenile offenders is explored. It is a concern echoed in the government's 1990 White Paper. And it is a concern which has a considerable history in the legislative provisions relating to the use of social information in sentencing juveniles.

Under the provisions of the 1969 Children and Young Persons' Act S. 9(1) and S. 9(2), local authorities are:

1 *empowered* to make investigations and provide the juvenile court with information relating to 'Home surroundings, school record, health and character of the person in respect of whom the proceedings are brought';
2 *required* to provide such information where the court requests it. Additionally, under S. 2 of the 1982 Criminal Justice Act (as amended by the 1988 CJA) a juvenile court should 'normally' obtain a report if it is considering the imposition of a custodial sentence.

Recent DHSS practice guidelines for social workers stress that

> A social inquiry report is prepared because an offence has been
> committed and the court seeks the help of the report writer in
> providing an explanation and thereby assist its decision making.
> DHSS 1987: 35

While the 1982 Criminal Justice Act and the recent White Paper have
moved away from the 1969 Act's attempt to place the 'welfare needs
of the child at the centre' (Harwin 1982), there has in fact been little
diminution in the emphasis on social background in sentencing juvenile offenders. What has been seen in the proposed legislation is rather
a shift in emphasis from the importance of social background as an
indicator of 'need' for state intervention in the guise of welfare support, to the importance of social background as an indicator of 'need'
for state intervention aimed explicitly at control (critical accounts of
the old 'welfarism' have of course exposed the difficulties involved in
making such a distinction – see for example Harris and Webb 1987).

Thus, although guidelines on social inquiry report provision have
swung from a broader concern with themes of 'deprivation and depravation' towards a narrower focus on the offending behaviour and
its control (Bottoms and Stelman 1989; Home Office 1986; DHSS
1987), the 'social background' remains in place as a backdrop for the
practice of justice for juveniles and for strategies of youth control more
generally. Indeed, the research discussed in this volume suggests that
in 1986 magistrates were already operating a 'moral justice' (cf. Parker,
Sumner and Jarvis 1989) whereby social information was used centrally as an indicator of need for control, and that *this was interpreted by
them as a concern with the welfare of the child*. The legislative provisions of
the 1969 Act in relation to social information were in practice being
interpreted in the spirit of the yet to be formulated 1990 White Paper.
This is a reflection of the centrality accorded to the family in 'diag-
noses' of offending behaviour in discourses ranging from politician's
rhetoric, through that of academics and practitioners to the apocryphal
'man on the street' 'represented' in the popular media. It also stands
testimony to the dangers of interpreting the policy process from above
rather than on the basis of empirical research into the perceptions of
how policies work out on the ground.

The social information issue in fact raises fundamental questions for
the whole juvenile justice process. It is not just a matter of providing
reports on juveniles, but of the whole way in which the social background is perceived in sentencing and the way in which images of the
social environment of offenders become incorporated into punishment practices.

The administrative genre in social information research

Yet, while much has been written about the development of juvenile justice generally in the United Kingdom, the social information question has not occupied a prominent place. The major themes of the critique of welfarism, the resurgence of 'just deserts', and the search for something beyond both of these, have been worked and reworked; the whole juvenile justice enterprise has been imaginatively situated within analyses of social control and surveillance, to the extent that a further exposition could only be superfluous here (see, for example, Parsloe 1978; Morris and McIsaac 1978; Morris *et al* 1980; Harwin 1982; Morris and Giller 1987; Harris and Webb 1987; Pitts 1988; Donzelot 1980; Garland 1985). The question of social information, however, and in particular the question of *sentencers' use of social information* has tended to be treated as something of a separate side issue. It has not been fully integrated into the major sociological, philosophical or policy debates in juvenile justice and has stagnated as a rather muddy backwater, empirically and theoretically underdeveloped.

As long ago as 1971, Philip Bean commented that 'We need a sentencing model which . . . takes account of the information given to the courts' (Bean 1971: 177). The social information debate, such as it was, remained within the confines of the relatively narrow worlds of the administrators and the practitioner–researchers for the next 15 years. Social information was treated as synonomous with the social inquiry report and the examination of the part played by social information in sentencing was typically restricted to the question of the effect of reports on sentencing outcomes.

Hence while attention was paid to some of the work concerned with social work ideologies and the production of social inquiry reports (Hardiker 1975; Paley and Leeves 1982) and some warnings were issued relating to the possibly damaging effect of welfarist social inquiry reports on sentencing, little was said about the need to research *magistrates'* perceptions of reports, and nothing was said about the question of social information more widely. The discussion lodged in the groove of concern with welfare professionals' report-writing ideologies. Even school reports were not discussed until Ball's research (1983) placed them on the agenda through her critique of confidentiality.

This dark age was of course relieved by a steady trickle of studies in the social inquiry report and sentencing tradition exemplified by Mott (1977), Hine, McWilliams and Pease (1978) and Reynolds (1982). A review of studies in this vein may be found in Thorpe (1979), Bottoms and McWilliams (1986) and Brown (1989). Despite the obvious quality of much of this research, the overall result was a mosaic of insights into the criminal justice system – supplemented by small-scale local evaluations (Brown 1989) – which left a vacuum at the heart of the social information question.

Concerned with the everyday pragmatic problems of managing resources and getting the job done, such research tended to be narrow in scope and short-term in nature. This was reflected in the studies produced, which necessarily divorced the use of social information from its everyday context, the complex day to day workings of the magistrates' court. In general these studies asked questions like 'what is the effect of social workers'/probation officers' recommendations on sentencing outcomes'?, sometimes with a supplementary question, 'what is the additional impact of social background information?' They were carried out – some in a crude, and some in a sophisticated manner – largely by correlating input (social information categories such as family background and recommendations made by agencies) with output (the sentencing decision), controlling for certain central variables (age of offender, sex of offender, offence and record, for example). The variance not accounted for by independent variables was usually assigned to recommendations or to social background categories, the resulting figure, whether a percentage or a correlation coefficient, being presented as a measure of the influence of social information.

The value of such studies has been that they have suggested that social background information provided in reports has some kind of influence on decisions which cannot wholly be accounted for by controlling for offence variables or even offence variables and social workers' recommendations. What they have not done is to elucidate the nature of that influence.

Parker and Giller (1981) have commented on some of the shortcomings of the administrative genre. The main problem for present purposes is that there is a sense of the post mortem about much of this research: after the fact, vital organs are examined for symptoms of the cause of death. We are left knowing little about how real magistrates construe social information in real situations or of the kinds of ideas and predispositions which magistrates carry into the courtroom with them. Magistrates tend to appear as shadowy figures performing sentencing exercises or ticking boxes alongside predefined categories. If we try to answer the question posed earlier – 'how do magistrates use social information in deciding on juvenile cases?' – how are we to do so without reference to the magistrate? If we have some evidence to the effect that, somehow, home background or a social worker's recommendation bears some relationship to the form of punishment meted out to a child, what does this mean? What is it, for example, *about* home background that suggests to magistrates the type and extent of punishment? How do documents such as social inquiry reports work? What the correlational studies have shown us is that social information is, somehow, being incorporated into sentencing decisions. But when? how? and why?

Attitudes, ideologies and the sentencing process

Broader studies of decision making *per se* in the adult and juvenile courts have probably contributed more to an understanding of the place of the social inquiry in the sentencing process, although they have not placed the social information issue at the centre of their analyses.

Stuart Asquith and John Hogarth have carried out two of the most detailed studies, the former in the Scottish and English juvenile justice system and the latter in the Canadian adult court. Asquith raised the point, ignored in many of the administrative studies that:

> In particular, the selective and interpretive activity of . . . panel members and juvenile magistrates – governed as such activities will be by their systems of belief – are seen as important determinants in the practical accomplishment of juvenile justice.
>
> Asquith 1983: 37

Asquith addressed the issue of *relevance*. Unless information was seen as relevant it would not be used by magistrates in arriving at their decisions. But relevance in turn was likely to be determined by the ideologies of crime and punishment to which magistrates subscribed. While Asquith concluded that it was the ideology of justice or welfare which differentiated information take up, Hogarth more individualistically argued that:

> Attitudes were closely associated with all aspects of the sentencing process. The end result is a remarkably high level of internal consistency between magistrates' perceptions of the world and their behaviour on the bench.
>
> Hogarth 1971: 343

For Asquith, then, the way in which magistrates view cases, the information which they see as relevant to a decision and the outcome of that decision, are shaped by their ideologies; for Hogarth, by their attitudes. Hogarth went so far as to suggest that information which was not consistent with a magistrate's attitude threatened his (*sic*) whole concept of self and would be filtered out by the magistrate as he struggled to maintain his identity. Relating this to the issue of social information use, what both studies have in common is their emphasis on the selectivity of decision makers in using information. Particularly important was sentencers' propensity to select information which accorded with their general orientation towards sentencing, whether at the attitudinal or ideological level.

These studies represented major stepping stones to a broader understanding of the relationship of social information to sentencing. It is necessary, however, to travel still further for a satisfactory analysis. Notions of an ideology or attitude 'held' by a magistrate are over-abstract, over-general and can result in the same problem as occurs in the administrative studies: the divorce of decision making from its live context. Giving magistrates sentencing questionnaires to fill in regarding the factors influencing their decision at the time of sentencing, as Hogarth did, does not restore such life. For an attitude or an ideology 'held' by a magistrate is only really interesting insofar as it is one instance of a framework of meaning emanating from the everyday world in which the magistrate lives and works. Goffman puts this well:

> Social frameworks . . provide background understanding for events that incorporate the will, aim, and controlling effort of . . . a live agency . . . what it does can be described as guided doings
>
> Goffman 1975: 22

Asquith's ideologies, and Hogarth's attitudes (as they themselves recognize but do not pursue) imply the importance of magistrates' commonsense understandings of everyday life, of the organization of their life world (Schutz and Luckmann 1974). If ideologies and attitudes are to be seen as determining the outcome of sentencing decisions they must be seen in their natural environment, locked into the commonsense realities and problems which exist for magistrates as they do their job. Such attitudes and ideologies may, indeed, be as much produced through the activities which magistrates routinely engage in as they determine such activities. Put simply, the kind of person a magistrate is may influence the way she or he works; but then again, the kind of work which she or he does influences the person she or he is or becomes. Nor should we necessarily accept that a person is static; for, as Macmillan discovered in his study of attitudes among motoring offenders, people can be notoriously fickle in their identities:

> One driver said . . . 'what I do depends on my frame of mind' . . . he affirmed that he tried to answer the [attitude] questions

honestly but he felt that much depended on his 'mood' when he
drove, and his mood varied from day to day . . .
Macmillan 1975: 138

The very process of engaging in an activity can influence the way in
which we feel about it; this has been well documented in relation to the
inscription of beliefs in rituals: as Althusser noted, 'move your lips in
prayer and you will believe' (Althusser 1969). Sentencing in the magistrates' court in particular is a communal activity surrounded by tradition
and ritual and it is necessary to understand that this forms the context for
the development of the magistrate's personal frame as much as she or he
imposes her or his personal frame upon the world. The views of magistrates thus need to be tied into their experience of their work, their
more general *weltanschaung*, and the routines of the courtroom.

Beyond the attitude: conventions and culture in information use

What is also implied by Asquith and Hogarth's studies without being
explored in detail is the notion of the interpretation of data as an *active*
process. If magistrates can be seen to actively select and filter information according to wider principles of whatever kind, then information
cannot be regarded as a thing-like entity which has some existence
independent of the process of interpretation.

What is information? Can it be regarded as something which exists
in documents such as social inquiry reports, which will be selected (or
not) as the 'case may be [seen]'? Research in the areas of information
science and media studies, both centrally concerned with the communication of messages, tends to reject this view (Swift, Winn and
Bramer 1979; Morley 1983). No message, whether visual, spoken or
written, can be assumed to have only one, unambiguous meaning.
Messages may indeed 'propose and prefer' certain meanings over others but the way in which those messages will be decoded by the
recipient can never be a foregone conclusion. Magistrates themselves
recognize this: as one senior magistrate commented, 'Magistrates will
read different things into reports'.

Barnes (1977) argues that actors accomplish this by constructing
representations from the data before them. A representation is simply a
picture, a way of framing the world out there: defendants' home
backgrounds may be represented as caring, good, chaotic, bad and so
on. A referent, by contrast, is the raw material to which the representation refers: for example, the actual offender, the actual lived reality of
the defendant's life.

A social inquiry report, of course, is itself a set of representations from which magistrates themselves manufacture further representations and so it is doubly distanced from its raw material. What is crucial for present purposes is that the raw material can *never* be faithfully reproduced. It is not a question of attaining objectivity. The very process of communicating involves the report writer or the magistrate in the business of interpretation, which shapes the reality of the defendant's background in a particular way. It is not only beauty which is in the eye of the beholder but a whole range of other human qualities.

What is it that governs the way in which the raw data will be shaped? Is it a purely random process, with every individual interpreting messages differently according to her or his particular idiosyncracies? Barnes (1977) has suggested something rather different: that interpretations are built up according to *conventions* which are closely allied to the practical objectives of actors and the activities in which they are involved. Phenomena are likely to be interpreted in a way which best furthers the task in hand and the kind of representations produced from data will depend as much upon the social position of the communicator/reader as they will upon the actual nature of the referents being interpreted. Hence, as Barnes argues, drawing on the work of Gombrich (1959; see also Bourdieu 1984), representations must be seen as 'relevant in various degrees to the ends or objectives of cultures or subcultures' (Barnes 1977:6). They are

> actively constructed conventions or meaningful cultural resources, to be understood and assessed in relation to their role in activity. Essentially this amounts to making representations analogous to techniques, artistic conventions, or other forms of culture.
>
> Barnes 1977: 9

Thus the arm in the nude or an anatomical diagram of an arm both relate to a definite reality: but neither is more 'true' than the other. The arm painted by Rembrandt and the arm in a medical textbook both have the same referent but are quite different as representations. The information they propose relates to the different worlds of the illustrator/medical student and the artist/art collector. Similarly, information 'about' the family background of the offender may be ordered around the interpretive conventions of psychiatry, sociology, social work, each of which might produce a rather different picture of that background from the other. Any representation implies a whole culture, embracing social relations which are produced and reproduced through the routine practical activities of its members. Its nature will relate as much to these activities as to the lived experience of the defendant's life.

Social information and social power: translating the defendant

Social relations, in turn, are not neutral but inherently political. They involve actors pursuing activities which, however unselfconsciously they are performed imply particular sectional interests of various kinds. Different actors within the juvenile justice system will not only interpret 'the facts' in different ways; they will also have an interest in persuading other actors to see it their way. Thus social workers and probation officers in communicating social information to the bench are proposing one version of the case; solicitors may be proposing a different version; magistrates, clerks, and defendants and parents themselves may also be involved in producing different images of the case in hand. Again it must be stressed that this does not necessarily involve conscious manipulation. It is rather that different actors within the justice system will be routinely operating according to differing conventions, which will in turn reflect structural differences in their social positions.

Hence, for example, the social background of an offender is not something that is simply given in a social inquiry report (SIR). Rather the SIR presents a set of representations about the defendant which seeks to promote a particular picture of that defendant for a particular purpose. Others are promoted by solicitors, the school, by defendants and by parents. The sentencing process is thus composed of a myriad of negotiations entered into by the various actors from different locations in the juvenile justice system. Every interaction of the courtroom, whether it is carried out face to face or via documents such as SIRs, constitutes such a negotiation. And in every such interaction the participants are seeking to ensure that their view prevails. This attempt by participants to win over the other players in the game has been usefully developed by Callon, Latour and Law into a 'sociology of translation' (Callon 1986; Latour 1986; Law 1986). To 'translate' the other participants is to *successfully get one's views accepted in the course of a negotiated outcome*. This involves, therefore, mobilizing a particular view of a person, thing or situation and making that view stick so that it comes to form the basis of an enduring belief or action. In the court context this would mean successfully articulating a particular view of offending which then became part of the conventional wisdom underpinning sentencing practices or successfully articulating a particular interpretation of a case in hand which would then result in a particular decision outcome.

The basic concept here is not difficult; anyone who has served on a committee will be familiar with the skilled tactician who always manages to ensure that his/her view prevails without appearing to use undue force. A sociology of translation is useful because it spells out explicitly the stages of the translation process and the tactics used by participants to try and effect successful translation.

Callon (1986) sees this as a fourfold process involving problematization, interessement, enrolment and the mobilization of allies. Each negotiator (whether solicitor, social worker, magistrate, clerk, parent, defendant) in a situation becomes a would be definer, a player who has an interest in getting a certain view of the case accepted by other participants. Thus, *problematization* involves the would be definers in establishing 'obligatory passage points' through which all messages have to be channelled. This may mean that a problem has to be represented in a certain way before it can be viewed as valid. In the context of the courtroom successful translation requires that a certain way of seeing juvenile cases be established as obligatory. This may mean that certain ways of speaking, writing or otherwise presenting a case are ruled out of court. Because the final decision rests with magistrates they have an advantage in the politics of translation: they can refuse to consider information which is not presented in an acceptable way and thus establish obligatory passage points. They are *potentially*, therefore, the most powerful of the would be definers. Problematization is central to translation because it acts as an already existing constraint on any actor who subsequently wishes to influence a situation ('if social workers want us to listen to them, they have got to write their reports in a realistic way').

The second tactic of translation, *interessement*, involves the formation of a holy alliance – a provisional coalition – between one set of would be definers and another in order to block out a common enemy – a potential challenge which would affect all the members of the coalition adversely, despite the disparity in their own interests. Magistrates may form such a coalition with solicitors, social workers, clerks and with each other: although in many senses all of these may be in opposition, they all have an interest in rendering defendants' and parents' cases which can be expeditiously and bureaucratically processed. 'Messy' cases are in none of their interests for they absorb resources and disturb the smooth running of the justice process. The common enemy is complication. Again magistrates are potentially the most powerful of the would be definers. Magistrates may indeed form a holy alliance with other officials in order to preserve the coherence of the process of justice, but they are in a position to call off that alliance at the point where it ceases to be congruent with their project of translation.

Thirdly, *enrolment* is precisely that – the enrolment of actors into compliance with interessement. Compliance may be gained through physical force but more commonly it is achieved through seduction ('look at the potential gains you will make from compliance'). Agency representatives, solicitors, parents and even defendants themselves must be to some extent drawn into an acquiescence with the rules of the game. Often it may be put to defendants that it is in their best interests to 'play the game': to play up to the image which will make sense to magistrates. Similarly, solicitors and social workers may enter into compliance by attempting to frame their representations in ways which will find favour.

The final tactic in the translation process is the *mobilization of allies*: what Callon terms a 'cascade of intermediaries' or spokespersons are mobilized who, because they are supposedly representative of many others outside the immediate situation, are taken to stand as proxy for those others in whose name they are said to speak. Magistrates, for example, may present themselves as intermediaries for the community; social workers may be held to represent the welfare of the child. This is crucial to translation because in establishing representatives, the would be definers effectively silence those who are represented, thus reducing the potential number of challengers to the view which they are attempting to make stick. To claim oneself as a representative, or to define someone else as a representative, is a way of investing the representative with a significance beyond the immediate situation. Again, this is easy to grasp in everyday terms; it is the attempt which most of us have made to legitimate our position by appeal to our status as representative of the person in the street: we may say 'it's commonsense that' . . . or 'everyone knows that', hoping thereby to add force to our point. This is no less than a technique of translation. We might be uncomfortably surprised if the people on the street actually made their views known! Thus as Callon points out, 'Who speaks in the name of whom? Who represents whom? . . . to speak for others is first to silence those in whose name we speak . . . (Callon 1986: 216).

Insofar as the four moments outlined above are successfully managed, then translation will be effective: a situation is successfully defined in a particular way and a particular version of reality is made, at least for the present, to stick.

The charting of success in the translation process can only be achieved empirically. In the present study magistrates were the most effective of the would be definers; but this did not prevent other participants in the sentencing process from making concerted efforts to translate magistrates.

Information, in its widest sense, is crucial to the translation process. For if, as we saw in the discussion of the creation of knowledge representations, information is actively produced from a mass of raw data 'out there', it is the translation process which will guide and decide the form the information produced from the data will take. If we recall that raw data may be counted as actors, as entities, as inscriptions, as the spoken word, gestures, pauses or tones of voice (at least), then the whole sentencing process may be seen as one in which it is necessary to commandeer the raw data into the service of successful translation: data is first displaced, then 'reassembled at a certain place at a particular time' (Callon 1986: 216) – reassembled to support a particular view.

Thus a situation in a juvenile court may be envisaged where the actual data conveyed by the defendant, whether embodied in her/his physical appearance or in the conditions of her/his life, may come into conflict with a way of seeing the case which is necessary for justice to be seen to be done. The power of the clerk, solicitors or magistrates is illustrated by their ability to deny the message which the defendant is attempting to convey and to transpose it into a more convenient form, as McBarnet has clearly shown (McBarnet 1981). It is necessary for the defendant either to be cast as the 'dummy player' (Carlen 1976) or for her/his message to be transposed, because the practical activity of the court cannot accommodate the defendant's reality. The analysis of translation is obviously a study of power; for the players who manage to make their view of the case prevail are effectively powerful. We are attempting to discover, as Law puts it,

> The methods by which actors and collectivities articulate conceptions of the natural and the social world and attempt to impose these on others and the extent to which these are met by success.
>
> Law 1986: 3

'Success' then, is power, in the sense used by Latour:

> Those who are powerful are not those who 'hold' power in principle, but those who practically define or redefine what holds everyone together.
>
> Latour 1986: 273.

Power is seen here not as something which can attach *per se* to the office (of magistrate, or clerk, of solicitor, of social worker): it is an effect of social activity which must be charted empirically. Thus to understand how magistrates operate in the translation process is also to understand how they operate within the social relations of power in the courtroom. Everything in the courtroom, everything that is spoken, written, seen, done, existent, is potentially a resource from which the decision maker can manufacture something which we may call information. What happens when the decision maker confronts this data and interacts with it in the process of sentencing, is the production of information. Magistrates have to manipulate the data out there in order to use it. They will screen out certain elements; scale down some aspects of the data and scale up others; they will schematize the data to make it more comprehensible to them; selectively highlight what they feel is crucial; these may be termed the practical techniques of translation (Law 1986).

The exercise of power through translation depends, of course, on classification. A representation, for example, of a 'chaotic' home background or a 'caring mother' or a 'basically good lad', is efficacious because it makes the case in question 'An instance of one or more kinds of entity, recognised by the culture whose resources are drawn on' (Barnes 1977: 5). Hence mothers may be classified into caring/ supportive, collusive, 'not interested'; 'lads' may be classified as anti-authority, basically good. The important point is that these are the categories of the would be definers; they exist for the convenience of communication, and as foci of negotiation; but they have little to do with the *actual* mother or 'lad'. They are the tools of translation. In being able to classify defendants and parents according to such categories, the objectives and priorities of the participants in the sentencing process are imposed upon complex individuals. Only by categorizing can decisions be made. Thus successful translation is achieved within the battleground of classification: the good/bad, the normal/abnormal (Foucault 1977). The social background of that object, the defendant and her or his family, becomes a pawn in the information games of the courtroom (cf. Carlen 1976). The actors in the courtroom are adopting the techniques of William Golding's protagonist in *Pincher Martin*:

I am netting down this rock with names and taming it. Some people would be incapable of understanding the importance of that. What is given a name is given a seal, a chain. If this rock tries to adapt me to its ways I will refuse and adapt it to mine . . . I will impose my routine on it, my geography. I will tie it down with names.

Golding 1979: 86

The courtroom is the rock for all the participants in its transactions. Sentencing in the juvenile court is about the negotiation of outcomes between magistrates themselves and between magistrates and agencies; the naming battles which form part of the translation process are the techniques which form the basis of this negotiation.

Reworking the information question: a study of six courts

The implications of this reworking of the information question are fourfold. First, the understanding of magistrates' use of information in sentencing has to begin with a magistrates' eye view of the sentencing process. Second, magistrates' views on the relevance of social information for sentencing have to be located in the wider framework of their routine activities within the arena of the juvenile court; within, loosely speaking, the organizational context within which they work. Third, information itself has to be seen as something which is *produced* by magistrates in this context as they decode the wealth of data which abounds in the courtroom situation. And fourth, a concern with the perceptions of magistrates, with the operational context within which they work, and with the process of magistrates' decoding of data, necessitates an analysis of the social relations of the courtroom, and of juvenile justice more generally, which is centrally concerned with the concept of *power*.

Thus the social information question is relocated from an issue of measuring the impact of reports on sentencing, to a perspective which places social information at the very heart of the sentencing process. Social information is not an addendum of sentencing activity; rather sentencing is conducted using social background representations as counters in a series of exchanges whereby all the actors in the process become would be definers, attempting to secure an outcome which is harmonious with their routine activities and the state of consciousness they occupy.

The study upon which this book is based was carried out in six English juvenile courts between 1985 and 1988. It began as yet another piece of social information and sentencing research but the initial informal contacts with magistrates and courts suggested that a more wide ranging approach was necessary. The importance of the theoretical concerns outlined above emerged as these contacts developed. Growing from these, the research design contained the following elements (see Appendix 1):

1 Gathering accounts from over 90 magistrates about information use, using relatively unstructured interviews (taped in most cases), wherever possible relating the discussion to specific cases.
2 Observation of cases in the six areas selected for study, (referred to in the text below as courts A–F for anonymity) aimed at identifying social background representations in use in the juvenile court through the interactions of solicitors, defendants and parents, clerks, magistrates, and welfare agency representatives.

3 Analysis of a sample of 122 social inquiry reports presented to the courts during the observation period.

A naturalistic orientation towards the data was deliberately adopted, the concern being with mapping information representations and their constitution within the decision processes of the court, so that 'The language used and the concepts and objects within the natural discourse are of greater importance than the opinion expressed' (Cain and Finch 1981: 110). No attempt was made to achieve the kind of abstraction of concepts for formal causal analysis which was carried out in much of the research discussed in this chapter. But neither should naturalism be taken to imply that the data 'speaking for themselves' (Cain and Finch 1981). What was attempted was a study of representations in the contexts in which they occurred and were applied through a series of processes within their institutional settings. Thus unlike many of the studies discussed above, the ascription of causal primacy to any one moment within the process of sentencing (its 'freezing' on an attitude scale or similar tool) was rejected. The relationship between the discursive formation and practice which the research sought to reveal was not the 'effect' of what is said on what is done but the mutual growth and intertwining of the two, the inscription of what is said within what is done.

Thus the concepts invoked by magistrates are not to be seen as reflections of attitudes, as external manifestations of an internal subjectivity. Instead, such concepts (the caring mother, the thoroughly bad lot) are continually to be defined in relation to each other and in the context of the situation in which they are used. A similar analytic process was used in observation sessions, to map the deployment of representations, to relate them to each other and to the part that they play in sustaining and reproducing the practices of juvenile justice.

The initial interviews followed a painstaking process of encouraging magistrates to identify the issues which they felt to be important in social information and sentencing. The interviewer tried not to ask overly specific questions but concentrated instead on guiding discussion by

- Seeking clarification of meaning, continually seeking confirmation that the interviewer's perception of what had been said matched the respondent's intended meaning.
- Seeking to elucidate what sources of social information were used, what kind of representations were invoked, what the 'ways of seeing' were, and how they related to practice. Frequently questions were asked along the lines of 'how does that help?'; 'why is that important?', 'what do you mean by?' However, care was taken

not to force the respondent to provide clarification if this was not readily forthcoming. For example, when asked why a particular aspect of the social background of an offender was considered important, a magistrate might reply: 'Well, I don't know really . . . it's a . . . *feel* you're trying to get . . .' To attempt to force the respondent further might not only appear threatening, but would also make him or her feel that they had to produce reasons whether or not she or he actually felt they were valid.

- Developing out from social information to broader issues in concentric circles. Questions regarding social information created ripples which led outwards to general issues relating to the sentencing of juveniles, key theories of offending and so on. Thus as social information representations were invoked in company with an account of practical activity, they were also invoked in the context of wider ranging statements. The interviews built on this tendency by not discouraging any attempts by magistrates to situate accounts and by encouraging the development of the issues thus raised. The technique was one of continually addressing the contexts of statements rather than seeking reasons for actions.

The main structuring device to emerge from the initial interviews was a shopping list of substantive areas raised by all magistrates:

1 social inquiry reports;
2 school reports;
3 defendant/parents in person;
4 solicitor's mitigation;
5 magistrates' own perceived knowledge and experience;
6 relationships with social services departments/social workers and probation service/probation officers and/or court officers;
7 the scale of offending against which the particular offence and the social information was set;
8 concepts of 'what it's all about', 'what we are trying to do' in the juvenile court, and 'what I'm here for' on the part of magistrates.

The aim was to chart the cultural conventions adopted by magistrates in the sentencing process, to analyse how these were mobilized in practice as magistrates attempted to translate defendants and professionals; and to understand the processes by which other would be definers − solicitors, agency representatives and defendants/parents themselves − attempted to enter into negotiations with magistrates and to translate magistrates to *their* version of how the case should be seen. This is the process of social information use in the juvenile court.

CHAPTER 2

From report to reader: magistrates and social inquiry reports

You are trying to . . . fit the pieces of the person together like a jigsaw puzzle . . .

Magistrate on the use of social information

This chapter will consider the nature of social inquiry reports as a text to be read by magistrates and will then shift the focus on to magistrates themselves and their perceptions of the role of reports in sentencing. Emphasis is placed upon the consumption rather than the production of reports and for this reason the analysis of social inquiry reports is not intended to be a formal or exhaustive content analysis. Instead the prevalent themes in reports which were identified by magistrates as particularly important are stressed, using illustrative quotations from the reports themselves.

Social inquiry reports: the conventions of report writing

While we shall be chiefly concerned below with the way in which magistrates interpret reports it is also important to recognize that the social inquiry report does not present the reader with a blank page on which to inscribe meanings according to whim. The social inquiry report may be said to 'propose and prefer' certain meanings over others (cf. Morley 1983), existing as a flexible resource to sentencers. It is therefore desirable to examine the way in which social inquiry reports are written before proceeding with an analysis of magistrates' reading of reports.

The social inquiry report does not simply or objectively reflect a real juvenile and the conditions of his or her life; nor could it. The report's raw subject matter is the individual who has become, through the processes of transgression and apprehension, a 'juvenile offender'. From the moment the individual enters the justice system she or he ceases to be a full individual and begins to become something less, a *category* of person about whom only certain 'facts' will be perceived as relevant. Hence the social inquiry report, far from being a description of a real person, *necessarily* displaces him or her through the processes of selectivity. Central to the theme of the present study is that such selectivity is not random but will rather be ordered around the conventions and assumptions of the authors.

Reports were found to possess a number of common themes around which a selective biography of the offender was ordered and which magistrates identified as central to the sentencing process. An examination of some of the conventional properties of SIRs will perhaps serve to illustrate these points and to indicate the typically preferred meanings of SIRs.

Selective biographies: major themes

In one sense the SIR is a narrative story in the tradition of realism. It does, as Wootton commented, turn the case into a human being (Bottoms and McWilliams 1986). Yet at the same time it turns the human being into a case. The SIR presents the offender's story; yet at the same time, much is left out of the story. Reports typically began with an introduction to family members with a few initial 'facts' to set the scene. Often semi-tabulated to assist rapid assimilation they provide a context within which to view the subsequent narrative.

Thus it is possible to ascertain immediately from the front page of most reports whether our characters are from the class of the 'deserving' or the 'undeserving' poor, working or on state benefits. One soon learned to anticipate the questions which would be addressed in this *mise en scène:* are there large numbers of offspring? Are there two parents of the same name, living at the same address or are there separated parents, cohabitees, half-brothers and sisters? Does the family emanate from a respectable area of town or from one of the 'trouble spots'? Is it a council house or owner occupied? Are the children squashed in an undesirable manner into too few bedrooms? Is the house kept clean and tidy and well maintained or are we facing the slovenly habits of the idle and feckless? Thus is the stage set for the working through of the major moral themes of the report: the 'good' or 'bad' family, 'good' or 'bad' home characterized by care and control or chaos and indiscipline.

A major theme of the body of the report was found to be the 'parents' tale'. This depicts a history of the parentage of the child. It may be a history of divorces, remarriages and cohabiting; of a 'caring' stable marriage or of something between the two. Emphasis was given to the relationships entered into by the mother, in whom a certain sexual licentiousness might be inferred and whose 'immorality' in that case was likely to be implied as a 'cause' of the defendant's generally anti-social behaviour:

> P. lived with her mother, who had . . . erratic relationships with a succession of men and for most of the time P. was left to fend for herself without boundaries of control.

> Mrs B. is somewhat self centred and there have been times when she has put her own needs first over and above those of the children . . . there have been several periods of domestic upset, change, and insecurity which might have been avoided.

Even where no history of the 'broken home' could be found the mother was characterized as generally blameworthy. This was frequently couched in the form of comment on her 'over-indulgence' or 'over-protectiveness':

> I formed the impression that D. was over indulged, especially by his mother.

> Mrs C. has always tended to be a more indulgent and over protective parent, and . . . W. has managed to manipulate this situation to his own advantage.

'Natural' fathers rarely received the kind of attention paid to mothers and tended to appear only briefly in the narrative unless they had 'serious drinking problems'. The *absence* of a 'stable male figure' was, however, usually commented upon. A father in steady employment was usually introduced approvingly, and so was one who was a 'disciplinarian' (the 'appropriate' male role to complement that of maternal 'ordering and sweet influence'). In this way it was implicitly assumed that the mother bears responsibility for 'failure' in socializing children effectively.

'Good' backgrounds were typically portrayed in the same stereotyped vein as 'bad' backgrounds:

> He belongs to a close knit family who have all been upset by his offending behaviour . . .

> Both Mr and Mrs S. present as caring, supportive parents . . . they have grounded L. indefinitely and stopped his pocket money . . .

Familial 'failure' was laid firmly at the door of the parents, particularly the mother. Educational 'failure', however, was never assigned to teachers or to the educational system. It was attributed to the attitudes and personality of the defendant:

> It was M.'s stubborn refusal to apply himself to attend [school] which predicted his removal firstly from home, then eventually to his placement at x . . . he is not without academic capability and would have attained more if his school attendance and diligence had been greater . . .

> His final term at [school] saw him absent from school on many occasions due to suspension for unruly and aggressive behaviour . . .

> [School staff] find J. lacks interest in his school work, is poorly behaved and can be aggressive.

An image is here presented of a downward spiral in the educational system, putting the defendant over as being beyond all bounds of control, for if the school cannot control him, then who can? 'As you can see, your Worships, J. is a boy on the edge of trouble in every area of his life'. Similarly 'failure to respond' to care institutions was portrayed as individual failure, not that of the social services department: 'Admission to care made little difference to K. and he was equally uncontrollable both in the Unit and in the educational setting . . .'

Indeed, the defendant may be presented as deliberately manipulating the situation:

> K. has done just enough to warrant a calculated gamble of his being allowed to return home . . . K. returned home on trial . . . offences were committed during this period . . .

Such histories were generally geared more to justifying the decision-making processes of the social services department than promoting an understanding of the situation and as such tended to obfuscate rather than illuminate the 'real' defendant. 'Good' responses to care institutions, moreover, were normally noted only briefly, whereas negative assessments were entered into in detail and were always individualized. Thus the portrayal of the defendant within the major controlling institutions of school and care shifts emphasis from familial pathology to 'badness'.

Judgements of 'badness' or 'goodness', a discussion of the character and attitude of the defendant, were always presented as authoritative statements in reports. There was never a subscript: 'but I might be wrong'. Again the emphasis lies on the failure of the individual, his or her inability to accept authority, his or her *intractability*, not only in terms of offending but in terms of general norms of conduct. The inequalities or constraints which the interview situation might impose are not acknowledged:

> On interview L. presents as a sullen young man with whom it is very difficult to hold a two way conversation . . . He does seem to be a determined individual who finds it difficult to accept authority unless it suits him . . .

> His attitude to reporting to me has not been particularly satisfactory and throughout the supervision order it has been felt that perhaps L.'s motivation towards keeping out of trouble has not been as good as it should have been . . .

L., in other words, is a headache, a problem case; he is 'hassle' who is wanted off the caseload. 'Positive' assessments of character and attitude tended to refer to the defendant's cooperation in interview, his/her possession of interpersonal skills, a willingness to 'open up', to be 'pleasant' and to change his or her behaviour:

> J. presents as a bright confident boy who is pleasant and co-operative in an interview situation . . .

> M. presents as a pleasant, articulate lad . . .

> N. is conversational, alert and a pleasant young man when he wishes to be . . .

It is likely that neither the positive nor the negative image bears much relationship to the actual personalities of these boys. What is important is their behaviour in an interview situation or their manageability from a casework perspective; the problems or promise that they hold out for the social worker.

Judgements of character or attitude of the defendant were often expanded upon to include the way in which she or he spent leisure time. Although occasionally reports referred to the *opportunities* afforded by the local area for leisure, the typical treatment of this theme again focused on individual *choice*:

> J. and his particular friends are liable to 'hang about' the estate. They have no leisure activities . . .

> D. has no real interests and spends his time 'hanging about the town' with friends, some of whom have recently been charged with D.

> C. has no particular hobbies or interests and spends most of his

spare time with his girlfriend, frequenting flats and lodging houses in the town . . .

In this way, what may be regarded as perfectly normal behaviour is classified as somehow threatening and deviant, clearly implying that a lack of structured leisure is symptomatic of an orientation towards delinquency. Youth clubs, football teams and army cadets are cited approvingly as instances of positive behaviour and an orientation towards conformity.

The narrative of the SIR thus operated its subject matter through a series of behavioural stereotypes which stressed the supposed pathology of offending behaviour, presenting a version of the 'failed' family and the 'failed' individual or vice versa. The extremes of the unmitigated disaster or the success story provide focal points between which all other stories can be situated. The unmitigated disasters are the no hopers for whom the report writer can see no rescue, no sign of a happy ending. They paraded a litany of broken homes, lack of maternal care, chaotic families, behavioural transgressions at home and school, academic failure and truculence. Such reports, although comparatively few in number, loomed as a shadow over all other stories, intimations of the potentialities contained within every case:

> There are massive problems in the marriage, which operates on a very low level of communication . . . mother is over protective and has thus placed herself in an easily manipulative [sic] situation. D. feels he should not be refused anything, and well realises his mother's weakness. With what seems to be gross parental mismanagement, he has become disturbed and confused and does not recognise any boundaries . . . running away from home, being rude and abusive . . . neighbours were making complaints of D. and he was attracting dubious characters to the home. D.'s ability to cope at [care institution] is being regarded in a fairly negative way, and at the present time . . . he is probably in need of more structure. He is totally incapable of organising his life, particularly his leisure hours . . . My feeling is that some salutory measure is necessary for this young man, and it may be that a short period of detention is necessary to effect this.

The above catalogue of disasters did not mention the circumstances of the offence nor the defendant's view of it. The narrative excludes any reference to the actual offending behaviour beyond the comment that 'He admits fully the offences for which he is before your worships today'.

In contrast stood the 'success stories', portraying a picture of a stable, caring couple with the man in employment and the woman a good housekeeper and mother:

Home Conditions

3 bedroomed terraced house. Owner occupied. Well maintained.

1 W. lives with his family in a large owner occupied terraced house . . . situated in the centre of town

2 Mr and Mrs C. have been married for 17 years . : . Mr C. is in regular full time employment and Mrs C. contributes to the family income from her part time work as a cleaner

3 Mr and Mrs C. impress as caring parents who want the best for their children . . .

J. has a good deal going for him at the moment. A good home, supportive parents, not the worst school record I have seen, and some sporting prowess. He has already begun to think about the transition from school life to work and at this stage I do not think he needs additional supervision.

Mr and Mrs B. are very caring and concerned parents . . . L.'s attitude to his parents is very changed and he now shows them the respect they deserve . . . L. is a good athlete and enjoys involvement in a number of sports. He is a good rugby football player and has played for his school and for [   ] Boy's team

Such extremes crystallize the chracteristics found to be common to the majority of SIRs: the portrayal of the social background as biography. The reports used the techniques described by Law (Law 1986) of 'screening out, scaling up, scaling down, cross sectioning, adding labels, and homogenising' in their attempt to persuade the reader to accept a certain version of the offender.

Thus vast areas of the defendant's life experience and views are screened out, such as the irrelevance of much of the school curriculum, the authoritarian nature of the school system, the bureaucratic inadequacies of the care system, the intolerance of teachers, the middle-class cultural prejudices of social workers, the lack of leisure and employment opportunities for working-class youth, the processes of arrest and plea taking . . . a whole range of structural and experiential factors of possible salience for the offence/s are filtered out by the internal 'logic' of the social inquiry.

This makes way for the scaling up of other elements and their organization into a narrative: the parents' marriage; the mother's failings in matters moral and maternal, educational performance and attendance; character and attitudes. Within the areas covered by the reports, the language itself produces an homogenizing effect which indicates conventional representation in its interchangeability across reports: defendants 'present as' a 'pleasant lad'; parents 'present as caring and concerned'; Mrs X. is rejecting of Y.; mother was 'overprotective'; father a 'disciplinarian'; Y. displays 'anti-authority attitudes', he is a 'follower not a leader' and he has agreed to work with us to 'look at his offending'.

The individual along with the complexity of his or her life, is actually destroyed by the report and is reconstructed as a defendant in a story which is comparable with every other story. The defendant is a construction fashioned from the private lives of individuals which may be set on a continuum from hopeful to hopeless, a construction which enables the individual to be categorized and judged in a fairly simple manner. There are clearly reasons relating to the intentions and social locations of authors, statutory guidelines, organizational issues, social work training and contrasting norms of practice across agencies and within agencies which explain the conventions adopted in writing SIRs for the juvenile court (cf. Donzelot 1980; Morris *et al* 1980; Morris and Giller 1983; Cohen 1985; Harris and Webb 1987; DHSS 1987). Certainly differences were found between social services department reports and the relatively small number of probation service reports examined. The latter tended to be more offence focused and somewhat less concerned with diffuse pathological origins of offending. This issue will be discussed further in the analysis of bench–agency relations (Chapter 5).

The primary intention here, however, is to consider magistrates' reading of reports and it is to their perceptions of SIRs that we now turn.

Magistrates and the reading process

As attempts to translate magistrates into a particular view of the case, how successful are social inquiry reports? How do magistrates interpret and use the kind of information which reports attempt to convey?

If reading is an active process involving the manufacture of representations by readers in accordance with their practical activities, situated within the social structure and culture of institutions, then the analysis must be directed at understanding how magistrates see reports as functioning in the juvenile court and the kinds of notions of relevance and usefulness which are contingently involved in their readings of SIRs. This necessarily forces an initial confrontation with the question of what sentencing juvenile offenders is about. The following represent the major themes which emerged from the interviews with magistrates regarding the ways in which reports were seen to function in the sentencing process.

Reports and recommendations

Firstly, reports were assessed in terms of their ability to act as guides towards an appropriate disposition. Only two magistrates in the sample echoed the following statement: 'It's not their business to make a recommendation. They shouldn't do it.' A further minority clearly felt less than enthusiastic about reports as providers of recommendations. This sentiment was usually expressed in the form of 'they could leave them off for me'. However, most magistrates welcomed, at least in principle, the practice of making recommendations and saw this as a *raison d'être* of the social inquiry report.

This emphasis on the recommendation needs careful examination. It should not be assumed that magistrates necessarily 'follow' recommendations; rather magistrates assess a recommendation on whether or not it is in line with their existing preferences. Magistrates' strongest and most consistent criticisms of reports related to unrealistic recommendations, even though these were conceded to be in the minority: 'My main problem with reports is that they recommend things which are just totally unrealistic. Not all the time, but quite often.'

'Realistic', on further investigation, invariably meant that the suggested disposition was considered to be 'too weak', 'erring on the side of leniency', 'not heavy enough' or, as one magistrate commented, 'too soft and wiffly'. It is a comment on the notion of individualized sentencing that magistrates rarely criticized reports for suggesting an inappropriate disposition, except in terms of the lenience/severity continuum. The majority of magistrates were found to work on the assumption that there is a tariff in the juvenile court and while some recommendations fell in line with this and so could be followed, others were ignored because they fell too far outside tariff brackets:

If the recommendation is totally invalid, then the rest of the report must be as well . . . all this sociological jargon, it stands or falls by its recommendation.

So very often you get a recommendation which just doesn't fit the bill at all . . . a CD when the boy had a CD a few months ago.

They recommend a probation order [*sic*] when I think that, there's no way they're going to make any headway . . . the time has come for some punitive measure.

At its simplest and most explicit, magistrates particularly in courts A and E made constant reference to the existence of the ladder or the scale up towards custody or the slippery slope or brink down towards custody: 'You are looking at a scale of offending. They go up the scale until there's nothing left.' Within the light and the heavy end of the scale, magistrates expressed some willingness to be flexible, within what they termed the 'large grey area' where the outcome was not obvious (for example, first offence conditional discharges (CDs) or inevitable (for example detention centre (DC) or youth custody (YC).

Well, you come to it in one of two states of mind. The first one is that they've committed something so heinous that there is only one penalty for them. That's in your mind firmly before you read it. And secondly, you just don't know what to do. You're either, as far as I can see, blinkered with what you want to do, either an absolute discharge, a conditional discharge, something right down the bottom of the scale, you don't think the police should have brought it . . . or at the top of the scale, there's only one solution, well, one sentence you can legitimately give, for the protection of the public and retribution, and to make sure that other people don't think they can get away with the same offence. In the middle of that, you've got a large grey area, you don't know what to do with them, and so you're looking for the report, and to my mind you want a minimum of two options . . . and the reasons for them.

Within the grey area, then, a recommendation could have potential to sway a magistrate either side of her or his provisional predilection depending on how the social data relating to the case was interpreted by the sentencer.

Hence, while in general the interviews with magistrates uphold the position taken by several writers that decision makers selectively interpret data in accordance with provisional decisions as to disposition (Hogarth 1971; Asquith 1983; Bankowski *et al.* 1987), some qualifications need to be made. In grey area or borderline cases, social background data could and did make a difference:

Sooner or later you come to the end of the road, but nevertheless, along the way hopefully, you can salvage something, and because of that, all the things that reports tell us, are relevant.

Social control indicators and SIRs

What is perhaps most interesting is the way in which magistrates may bring other information into play at this point: the failure of control may be judged not only on the perceived seriousness of the offence or on recidivism but on images of the social background of the offender.

Social background representations were used by magistrates for indications that something could be 'salvaged': that the defendant was still within the boundaries of control. Conversely, once an offender has reached the 'slippery slope' (particularly if reporting agencies themselves have 'washed their hands' of the offender) this search would be abandoned: all data would be taken to corroborate what sentencers believed to be already obvious: that the child was out of control, a hardened offender. More specifically, magistrates talked of a search for 'potential'; 'ability'; 'something to work on'; 'something positive' or 'something to build on' in the background data. This was part of a process of distinguishing 'hard core' offenders from those 'something might be done with': 'In the end you are talking about a very small minority of hard core offenders . . . reports help us to distinguish.'

Magistrates appeared to assess cases on a basis similar to the premises of control theory (cf. Hirschi 1969). In reading reports they looked for signs of attachment, commitment, involvement and belief, their sociological assumptions resting on the premise that weak social bonds are the key causative factors in deviant behaviour. The term control indicator is thus intended to convey the sense in which magistrates typically searched for and picked up on data which suggested to them that the child's bonds with 'upright society' were still to some extent intact. Either recidivism, a serious offence or evidence of weak bonds even in the absence of recidivism or seriousness, could be taken as an indication that the child was loosened from the fabric of social integration. The response to adverse control indicators is, of course, up tariff movement. In this sense there is a continual interplay between offence and social data rather than a playing off of welfare and justice factors. The use of control indicators, in other words the invocation of a scale of social integration, enables magistrates to solve their practical problems of sentencing: the need to take offence and social background data into account in the classification of offenders along a continuum of dispositions from discharge to custody.

In this situation it is easy to see how report provision may help to accelerate up tariff and so fulfil the prophecy that offenders will become classified as hard core. Where magistrates find adverse control indicators in grey area or borderline cases, an up tariff movement is likely to occur so that *subsequent* court appearances display failure of response to a 'stronger' disposition:

> A small financial penalty might have been in line had we thought that the father might have made it a penalty to him, but what the report said all pointed to the fact that that wouldn't happen, he needed something from outside [2 concurrent attendance centre orders].

Similarly in the case of a boy charged on a first court appearance with fiddling small amounts of money from ticket machines, adverse control indicators had contributed to an attendance centre (AC) decision. The AC order was then breached, and a DC order was imposed (this case is discussed further below, but it should be noted that adverse control indicators were provided not just by the SIR, but also by the school report, the breach of the AC order itself, the reporting police officer, and the justices' own knowledge of the family).

While the influence of other sources of social data should not be underplayed it is clear that the SIR does act as a *distinct* resource from which magistrates actively manufacture images of 'controllability':

> Conclusions form in the mind as one reads . . . if all the children are offending it suggests the need for intervention, that the parents aren't managing.

> Your mind starts going in a certain direction and you absorb information within parameters . . . a report isn't the only thing that influences you, to the fore is the offence and the previous convictions. You look at the potential of the child and the report is used to make things gel more. You look for indicators . . . the report can affect a good deal . . .

The use by magistrates of control indicators constitutes the crux, not only of social inquiry report use, but of the importance of social information in general.

Compare the account given by the magistrate in the case of the boy who fiddled the ticket machine (referred to above) with Foucault's comments:

> A whole micro-penality of time (lateness, absences, interruptions of tasks), of activity (inattention, negligence, lack of zeal) of behaviour (impoliteness, disobedience) of speech (idle chatter, insolence) of the body (incorrect attitudes, irregular gestures, lack of cleanliness) . . .
>
> Foucault 1977: 178

You saw the attitude of the boy this morning, in the report it had said that he had no intention of listening to what his mother or the police or the court had to say, it's very important. That we get the boy or girl's attitude to the offence . . . it's a form of rebellion . . . but it's gotta be monitored and corrected hasn't it because you can imagine a boy like that going further through life, I mean he's going to end up in prison as a dead cert isn't he? It was his appearance to us. He just sort of looked at us as if we were nobody to be dealt with . . . I mean . . . by the record it was a very minor offence, there's tons of youngsters do it . . . and then having said that, the family, I think, are . . . noted.

Magistrate, court E

Magistrates are engaged in an overall project of seeking to preserve and impose discipline (cf. Foucault 1977 and further discussion in subsequent chapters) on youth and it is within this project that the practical problems of sentencing through classification are addressed by magistrates. While the tariff is evidential of the fact that justices operate within a classic legal mode of penality the project of discipline frames the allocation of offenders within this. Social inquiry reports as a knowledge resource for these allocation activities operate centrally through control indicators.

The SIR as an explanatory account

A third role played by reports in the processing of juveniles is in the rhetoric of diagnostics: with the exception of a number of sceptics, magistrates viewed one general function of SIRs as to be explanatory. Magistrates continually stressed 'explaining offending' as a justification for the relevance of a wide variety of background data. They said of the SIR:

It helps to explain why its happening.

It helps you understand how he got into that state.

It's all part of the background. You are trying to get a picture.

It [SIR] helps you understand what makes the individual tick

Some justices – more so in courts B and C than elsewhere – made the leap in a general sense from diagnosis to treatment: 'If you know whats causing it maybe you can do something about it.'

In practice this usually referred back to the question of control indicators. Magistrates typically located such 'causes' as the disintegration of family stability leading to under-socialization or emotional disturbance and a consequent lack of control. The notion of using a diagnosis of offending as a basis of action is, in magistrates' views, primarily a question of introducing stability, discipline and regulation where it is seen to be lacking. 'Looking for causes' remained at the level of individual/familial pathology and the supposed consequences of that for social (dis)order and property:

> We've got to try and see why they're doing it and it nearly always comes back to home life . . . they just haven't got that kind of support, the family group is just completely disintegrating really.

> It helps explain why its happening. Sometimes you get quite shocked. Kids outside of their parents' control, roaming the streets at night. You couldn't make a decision without some kind of information.

Very rarely did magistrates mention any broader economic, structural or institutional factors which might result in children appearing before the court, such as material deprivation, lack of viable opportunity structures or policing practices or even community economic organization. A small number of justices mentioned unemployment, typically in the context of the 'devil making work for idle hands'. One magistrate, however, attempted to set offending in the context of material deprivation and frustrated expectations:

> My colleagues are so out of touch. They say, 'there was unemployment in the 'thirties, and it didn't make us into criminals'. But it wasn't the same, we weren't living in a consumer society. Whatever you do, it's a dead loss. We're just part of the system which some people come into contact with. You don't have much choice as to what you can do. I live right in [x] and I see it all around − if they tripled social services it wouldn't do any good, these people aren't ever going to work, and they look at it as though . . . they've got to work, it's a kind of culture round here, lads grow up to expect they'll be earning and going out to pubs drinking under age with their mates, acting like adults . . . And it's different to the 1930s, we're living in a consumer society, there's things you've got to have.

This magistrate's account engages questions which the majority of justices, where they mentioned them at all, skimmed over with standard stereotyped responses (as this respondent points out). The central point here is that if magistrates do attempt to engage seriously with structural, economic or general cultural phenomena in crime causation this would produce a state of helplessness and a sense of futility which could threaten the magistrates' performance of their role in the juvenile court:

> Whatever you do it's a dead loss . . . you don't have much choice . . . if they tripled social services it wouldn't do any good . . . you just go up the ladder until there's nothing left.

> In certain areas of town that particular group will all be involved in the seacoal trade, or scrap . . . and you see, they are never going to change, now what do you do with anybody like that, because they're just going to go back into the same environment and they're going to do exactly the same as they've done all the time, pinch scrap or deal in scrap, just to make a living, do the seacoal or whatever.

> There's a general feeling of malaise in the town really which comes back to the unemployment . . . I mean the weaker ones of them are going to go to the wall . . . a lot of it is the devil finding work for idle hands and it's very very sad . . .

Keeping deviance out of the broader social structural context and within the bounds of pathology and culpability operates in the juvenile court to enable magistrates to carry out their duties in a manner consistent with the existing practices of the court. The range of dispositions available are essentially punitive and aimed at controlling individual behaviour at an individual/familial level. As such they can take no cognizance of social structural imperatives beyond the 'failure' of the family or the 'failure' of the individual.

Magistrates' emphasis on the SIR as a diagnostic tool utilizes the language of 'moral orthopaedics' (Foucault 1977) to achieve some congruence between their felt obligation to espouse both reformatory and retributional approaches while avoiding further enquiry into 'causes and cures' of offending. A more penetrative analysis of the latter than that provided by the SIR would take magistrates beyond the scope of their ideological positions, their typical practices, indeed, their statutory powers and so would be felt as threatening. In this context it is interesting to note that the magistrates who offered the sceptical view of their role were not case hardened cynics but relatively new justices of less than 18 months standing who, it might be argued, carried more of the 'outside world' in their analytical baggage. They had not yet become enclosed by the insulated complacency which was characteristic of some of the longer serving members of the bench.

The SIR as a mitigation address

Magistrates explicitly stated on occasion, particularly in courts E and A, that reports in practice could be seen as mitigation:

> You need the background information as a mitigating factor really because that's what the report's there for, that's why the solicitors go by it.

> It's now often in lieu of what the advocates should say.

The Clerk in court E was even more explicit on this than his bench:

> Of course they are mitigating documents. A good solicitor could do away with the need for the SIR in many cases. I don't think it matters, so long as every one knows that's what they are.

Not all magistrates who recognized the report as mitigation felt that this was a legitimate function:

> There's always this attitude on the part of the social worker that they have to take the side of the defendant . . . they shouldn't do that, they've got a solicitor to do that.

The relationship between the SIR and mitigation is reflected in the organizational procedure of courts A and E where solicitors were not normally expected to address the bench in mitigation if the magistrates agreed with the recommendation:

> We tend to read the reports, tell the solicitor we agree with the recommendations, and if he's got any sense he'll sit down.

This view of the SIR prevailed less strongly in courts B and C, or at least was not regarded as routine in the same way. Thus courts in E and A, and to some extent in D, a range of background data about the offenders' family circumstances or health might be regarded as mitigating factors irrespective of the intentions of the report writer in including such data. It is instructive to compare the official guidelines on SIRs and mitigation with magistrates' perceptions:

> Do not describe the offence in terms of mitigation. This is the responsibility of the defendant's solicitor.
>
> DHSS 1987

> I wouldn't use the solicitors' information in migitation, not in the juvenile court, I'd be looking much more in to the background, if its a good report.
>
> Magistrate, court E

Thus in the same way that magistrates coopted the diagnostic discourse of social workers to legitimize their punitive activities on occasion, they could equally coopt such discourse as mitigation.

In this emphasis on legitimation and control little attention has been paid to the notions of 'treatment' or 'rehabilitation' in magistrates' accounts of the functions of social inquiry reports. This is not because magistrates did not mention such categories but rather because on analysis those categories collapse into issue of control, as does the notion of individualized sentencing. Thus, as has often been pointed out, essentially damaging and punitive sentences such as DC become justified on the grounds of individual need: but the 'need' is perceived to stem from a lack of integration into the 'appropriate' normative structures of family, school and community which are seen to be the bases of discipline and useful citizenship:

> Well, I think in terms of does this child particularly need for instance, say, a short, sharp, shock, or, does he need some building up of his background . . . if his background is extremely poor and I think the poor kid hasn't had a chance anyway from the start, perhaps what he needs is the help of some stable adult, . . . thinking immediately in terms of a probation officer, or some sort of intermediate treatment, something that's going to build up the character . . . most of the time they [aims of sentencing] fall in to place, they don't conflict, inasmuch as when you decide what's best for the child, it often means perhaps, er, sending them away . . . that's a punishment . . . if it doesn't mean sending them away, but putting them on probation, there's an element of punishment in that, in that it ties down his activities somewhat and he has to be answerable to somebody . . . but the important side of it is that he's being shown and directed by somebody who has his well being at heart, that's the main thing.

It is when control is seen as having broken down that the need for 'treatment' is seen as particularly strong, usually in terms of removing a child from the 'contaminating' influence of an 'inadequate' family and providing him or her with much needed 'structure' and 'discipline'. Moreover, it was clear that many magistrates believed in the role of disposals within their power as attempts to reform; they continually referred to sentences as 'working' or 'not working'. This broadly fitted in with the notion of the tariff, as the following typical comments indicate:

> No way would we go for AC a third time. A second maybe if the first hasn't worked, but not a third time.

> If it didn't work the first time it's not going to work a second time.

> If that doesn't work, maybe he needs something stronger.

Thus in real terms there often seemed little to choose between removing a child from a 'bad' background for punitive or treatment reasons. As one magistrate atypically pointed out: 'We're very limited in what we can do, really. They're all punishment things, we can't just refer somebody to a child guidance agency or whatever.' The major difference between magistrates was not whether they saw cases in punishment or treatment terms but how far they would be willing to extend the tariff and their preferences for particular types of disposals. Hence for those who were willing to hold out until the 'inevitable', social inquiry reports could be used to identify control indicators for a child's ability to respond to supervision or alternatives to custody.

Finally, magistrates appeared to be seeking, for no clearly defined reasons, something from the SIR which they called a 'general picture':

It's all part of the whole . . . ethos you are trying to get at, to fit the pieces of the person together like a jigsaw puzzle.

It's a picture. You're trying to get a picture.

Trying to get inside the person, to understand what makes them tick.

Concomitantly, magistrates could express criticisms of reports with reference to these terms:

Well, . . . this morning's lot I found a bit thin somehow

This morning, the clerk said they were surfacey, and I thought they were.

It seems here that magistrates are responding to documents which are primarily structured in a narrative form, encouraging the telling of a story about an offender. Indeed, magistrates themselves not infrequently perceived the SIR in terms of 'telling the offender's story'. These justices stressed the inarticulateness of the offender and the 'unnatural' environment of the courtroom, so that the SIR was seen as placing the child in his or her 'natural' context as a means of access to the 'real' person. This is significant when we recall the selectivity of reports in producing biographies. The perceived need for the report to function as anthropology reflects the us and them situation of offender and sentencer, the social distance which was stressed by one justice:

Being local, one has a spatial knowledge of the community, but one's social knowledge is limited, terribly limited.

In this sense the report operates along with other features of juvenile processing to reinforce the separation of magistrate and offender as two essentially different beings. The 'real' person is reconstructed through the social inquiry report and magistrates, interacting with the typifications contained in SIRs, produce for themselves a story about the offender. The story contains all the essential features, organized in an understandable way, to enable the business of sentencing to be undertaken: explanations, control indicators, mitigating circumstances, need for . . . structure, discipline, guidance. All these are components of the process of organizing and ordering data to render it up as relevant information in the accomplishment of justice. The story enables magistrates to achieve a measure of harmony between their lay typifications of offenders and offending, the organizational processes of the court and the structural imperatives of the penal sanction system.

> We use the social worker as a channel of communication, like Teletext; we use it to get as much information as possible, the person behind the headlines . . .

Thus the social inquiry report operates as an instrument of surveillance but not in the simple sense of gaining direct access to the actions and meanings of offenders and their families. Rather the SIR colludes in producing a mythological representation of 'the offender' which is amenable to the disciplinary processing forms of action constituted in and through the juvenile court.

The lack of any strongly directive and explicit structure in reports renders them ineffectual in challenging magistrates' routine activities. Pathological data in particular colludes with magistrates' search for control indicators on which the lenience/severity continuum chiefly rests or alternatively may result in such data inappropriately being seen as an attempt at mitigation. The decontextualized nature of the pathology also means that the structural and institutional factors which may be relevant to an understanding of offending behaviour are omitted, reinforcing magistrates' tendency to individualize offending behaviour.

In face to face exchange of data – as in conversation – participants continually modify the way in which other participants interpret information, correcting what they perceive as the other's misinterpretation or else reinforcing a correct interpretation. Report writers, however, (unless consulted in court) do not have the opportunity to engage in this negotiation of meaning so that the clarifying process is undertaken by the magistrates and interpreted as far as possible to be congruent with the immediate and broader interests of magistrates in their regulatory activities. The potential of any report to be influential lies in its ability to be directive and resistant to such reconstruction as far as possible. For the most part, however, the reports were found to reinforce rather than challenge magistrates' existing predilections.

CHAPTER 3

Is mother on the booze?
Social background, control and
the sentencing process

Chapter 2 emphasized the importance of control indicators in magistrates' interpretation of social data. The present chapter will concentrate on a more specific analysis of the content and implications for sentencing outcomes of the control indicators which magistrates actively manufacture from SIRs in the course of the sentencing process. The task thus lies in describing the control indicators and in relating these in more detail to magistrates' routine activities.

Control and the family

Magistrates unanimously stressed that the first and paramount object of their reading of social inquiry reports was to gain information about the family background of the offender: 'I think the family background's terribly important. It's the first thing I look for without exception.' The homogeneity of magistrates in this respect is clearly an obvious point, given that social inquiry reports focus almost entirely on the family and situate the offender and offending clearly within some kind of family context. It is the precise signifiers within that category which are of interest. In the interviews a good deal of time was given to exploring exactly what it was about the family which was of importance to magistrates and why. Without exception, 'home background' was seen as the causative factor in offending pathology:

> It all comes back to lack of control. For that reason the family background's important.

> Mainly to find – maybe it's not right, but my feeling is you've got to find A. the home background, because I'm a great believer that the home background has a lot to do with it.

However, they stressed a number of core categories of family background information which were deemed to be of central importance
to decision making and these core categories shared common threads,
relating to a notion of family stability which was seen to impinge in
central ways on the behaviour of the offender:

> I think what we want to know about is what's the home like as a
> home, what are the parents like and what response does the
> child have to the parents, is home just somewhere he goes for a
> meal and goes straight out, or do they act as a family . . . do they
> physically take any interest in the boy at all, apart from . . .
> physically being his father and mother. Those are the sort of
> things I'm looking for.

> The parents' relationship, it's very important, very significant in
> the child's . . . I mean . . . invariably there's some breakdown
> there, isn't there? It's the first slippery slope without any doubt.
> So many of these people come from broken homes, almost
> invariably . . . second marriages, stepfathers, stepmothers.

The accounts reproduced above pose two alternatives: the stable,
caring, well regulated, well integrated home and the chaotic, uncar-
ing, disordered home. These images occurred repeatedly in magistrates' accounts of their search for information about the family
background. Magistrates varied mainly in their choice of language to
describe their information search on family background, rather than
the type of information which they sought. Some magistrates would
stress affective relationships while others would refer more directly to
control:

> You are looking to see what behavioural patterns there are in the
> family, the level of supervision and discipline, the parental control.

> I want to know if it's a caring home, if they are well looked after
> at home, what support they are receiving at home . . .

The distinction between care and control did not generally exist for
magistrates and in practice the two statements above amounted to the
same thing. The continuation of the second account is given below:

> But 'caring' as it's put in a report usually means they give them
> loads of pocket money. To me caring is knowing where your
> children are, it's the level of control that's important – like a 15,
> 16 year old out all night! I want to know, do they set times
> when they must come in and who they're associating with. Kids
> are in court because parents don't take an interest.

The concept of family stability on which magistrates placed such emphasis, then, clearly has several facets. As a core concept through which magistrates undertook their search for control indicators, it merits exploration in some detail.

The first facet of family 'instability' is the 'marital breakdown'. In magistrates' perceptions many of the children who appeared before them on criminal charges come from 'broken homes' and magistrates made a causal inference from this to offending:

> The majority are from one parent families – often their mothers and sisters can't handle them.

> Family background is very important . . . The lady today was divorced. You want to know then, does the father keep in touch, are they caring parents, what are the home conditions like, do the parents shown an interest and keep in touch with the school?

> Instability plays a big part. So much of it, it crops up all the time, often they've had three or four sets of parents.

> There are common influences in offending, frequently broken homes are the cause, and its important to have an impression – you might have a twelve year old out at 2 am offending while his mother's working as a barmaid.

> It's important to know the stability of the relationship between the parents – so often it's due to absent fathers.

> You want to know the family background because children have got to have two good parents who have a good relationship with each other and with the child.

Magistrates thus used SIR data on marital history to construct an image of continuity/discontinuity, of stability/instability and of mother/father roles. Marriage breakdowns were seen as particularly important because they were seen to involve a disruption of gender roles implicit in their images of the stable family and also, to a lesser extent, because conflict with a non-blood parent was seen to be a potential cause for a lack of authority.

Frequently magistrates would generalize from marital instability to a wider sense of chaos:

> What chance do such kids have, growing up in delinquent homes, broken homes? They are destined for crime. It's a culture of criminality, they are conditioned to behave in an anti-authoritarian way. Now, how do you start on rehabilitation?

Information about family background is important . . . the level of control in particular . . . there is a pattern in so many juvenile cases, the mother's and father's names are different, or one parent families. If all subjects came from honest, god-fearing families, we wouldn't have the problem.

The ideal family was thus seen to be one where two natural parents fostered a strong, integrated relationship with children and acted out the expected parts of father and mother. The requisites of playing the part well were continually stressed by justices in their accounts of building up information about an offender's family background:

You want to know, how does the family live as a unit, the role of the father. This is what is of crucial importance, – whether both parents are at home, what part the father plays in home life, what does the mother do.

It does help . . . if you get the picture that mother is the one who stays in every night of the week and father is down the pub every night . . .

You want to know for example if the father is interested in him. It sort of affects a young person's behaviour if father is in the club drinking all day.

Is the mother on the booze, or is she caring?

Magistrates' search for social information was thus inextricably tied up with the perceived pathology of offending and this set the agenda as to which data would be considered relevant – the agenda of social control indicators. The emphasis on family stability is central because the breakdown of such stability, the collapse of the moral order of the family, were seen as the preconditions for the breakdown of the social order in general.

What is being expressed here appears to be a somewhat Hogarthian image of the working-class family at its worst: central concepts are invoked of disorder and lack of moral fibre. The extensiveness of this image among the social control vocabulary of justices cannot be over-stressed. Whether in a milder or more extreme form, the 'moral dangers' to which working-class children are purportedly exposed were continually rehearsed by magistrates as a central referent for the manufacture of information.

Apparently welfarist considerations of family relationships almost inevitably came down to their relationship with the level of control over rebellious youth (and the putative future citizenry). Family instability was seen to entail several dangerous trends. First, a lack of power over the child in terms of the parents' ability to enforce compliance with regulations and to exercise surveillance: 'I like to know how the person relates to the parents and parental discipline and control' 'Do they know where their children are?' Second, family instability was seen to involve a lack of authority over the child in terms of parents' ability to command a child's respect for them and to the values of respect for property and authority figures in general:

> In a lot of cases, the parents have reached the stage where they're unable to discipline them.

> You want to know about discipline . . . whether they are taught respect for other people and for property.

Third, justices pointed to the unstable family as involving a lack of commitment on the part of the parents to providing an atmosphere of moral rectitude and emotional stability which would be conducive to fostering these successful authority relationships (the 'honest, god-fearing, family'):

> The attitude of the parents to their children is important and what kind of influence they may have.

> You want to know how the family sees the offence.

Specific indicators in social data which magistrates used to assess defendants and their families in these terms were numerous. Commonly taken as 'negative indicators' (that is, bad influences) by magistrates included:

- the presence of offenders in the immediate or extended family;
- the 'single parent';
- lack of a father figure;
- an 'over-protective' or 'immoral mother';
- alcoholism;
- problems in relationships with step parents;
- parents not knowing the whereabouts of their offspring;
- parents' inability to get children to school;
- working mothers, particularly where involving evening work such as bar work;
- a home not deemed to be 'well kept';
- financial irresponsibility (e.g. an over-preponderance of HP agreements);
- unwillingness or inability to punish children for their transgressions, particularly through deprivation of liberty (curfews) or financial penalties (stopping pocket money);

- a lack of appropriate concern about the offending behaviour by parents.

  Conversely, positive indicators were:

- 'natural' parents in a long standing marriage;
- a husband in work with a full-time housewife;
- strong involvement between father and son, especially involving mutual leisure activities such as fishing or football;
- a 'well regulated;' household (i.e. demonstrating 'good standards' of housewifery/domesticity – 'does she keep a nice home?');
- parents maintaining contact with school;
- a strong manifestation of concern on the part of parents, especially willingness to cooperate with agencies and the courts and to actively assist the court in applying sanctions.

The vision of the stable family invoked here is clearly largely a cornflake packet stereotype peculiarly inapplicable to the realities of contemporary family structure (Family Policy Studies Centre 1985). Fairly normal events in the lifecycle of a family, such as divorce, remarriage, cohabitation, periods of tension, stress and instability between family members, are redefined as pathologically significant. The yardstick of the stable family is also deeply gender and class biased and parallels the sexist paternalism on the part of Scottish sheriffs recorded by Carlen (Carlen 1983a). The mother is invested with the duties of nurture, good example through virtue, good housekeeping, and provision of emotional stability. The father is expected to wield patriarchal authority (physically if necessary) and to involve sons in neophyte manly pursuits such as fishing and football. The social cement is embodied for magistrates in their version of a patriarchal family structure conforming to the closed and narrow world of suburban middle class values. Deviance from gender roles within the family ('immoral' or 'boozing' mothers, 'workshy' or 'weak' fathers) is seen as indicative of a weakening in the social bonds which were seen by justices to tie a child into conformity.

Control and leisure

Second only to magistrates' stress on information about family background was the emphasis placed on the data in the SIR relating to the offenders' leisure time. This has to be set in the context of non-school attendance and youth unemployment. The majority of offenders appearing before the court during the observation period were, if not still at school, unemployed. Again, magistrates' concern with leisure time was centrally related to their concern with the susceptibility of the offender to control and, at a more general level, with the perceived consequences for social order of unsupervised, unstructured leisure.

Juvenile crime was typically perceived to be closely linked with freedom of movement: 'the devil makes work for idle hands' recurred frequently in the accounts given by justices as did an abhorrence of 'children roaming the streets'. 'Useful' leisure was consistently defined as structured activities which served to integrate the young person into the ordered world of adults and inculcate him or her with the proper values of community and respect for authority. Atomistic activities such as 'hanging around' on street corners, watching videos, playing on fruit machines etc., were generally considered to lead to offending.

> It is important to know whether they have hobbies, use their leisure time constructively, if they're a member of scouts for example, or a boys' club, or cadets, or even if they've got any constructive hobbies like angling or fishing.

> Whether they have interests or just slouch around all day – it's useful to know.

> There are lots of young people now with a lot of time on their hands, and it's important to know how they're spending it, whether they're doing anything useful.

> If I saw a kid was training for . . . rugby, or karate, say, I would put that down as a plus. It means the kid has taken conscious steps to use their time in an acceptable, useful, constructive way . . . I was chairman of the local football club and I came across several instances – it offers a way of rehabilitating, gets them into the idea of unselfish enterprise . . . use of leisure time can be used as a pointer to a kid's redeeming features.

While clearly secondary to the search for familial control indicators, magistrates strongly valued the perceived integrative function of structured (= constructive) leisure and would seek data relating to this. 'Positive' indicators were taken to be involvement in the kinds of activities outlined above, or excellence in a particular sporting activity, and several magistrates commented that SIRs 'did not give them enough' of this kind of data.

'Negative' indicators were taken to be unstructured, unsupervised activity, 'slouching around', particularly in the company of other young people regarded as 'anti-social'. Thus in court D, a popular seaside resort, justices were particularly critical of the tendency of local youth to spend their days 'hanging around' on the sea front, playing on the fruit machines; while in court E, an urban metropolitan area, 'aimless' riding around on the public transport system was regarded with particular disapprobation. In court A, an area of particularly high unemployment, but with a large modern shopping centre, 'hanging around in groups under the town clock' was seen as a particularly dangerous activity.

Hence specific local conditions provided a focus for justices' negative evaluations of how youth spent its time; but ultimately the perceived problem was the one of the threat of (unemployed) youth to public order and private property. Because of this, any nascent ('constructive') interests which justices perceived in the SIR data could be seen as 'something to build on' in the search for effective control. Activities which took place within the context of adult dominated organizations where defined as constructive. Activities taking place outside such organizations tended therefore to be defined as disorganized, in the broadest sense – particularly if those activities were not adult led. The concept of (adult) organization is thus invoked as an integrative principle against which juveniles are assessed. Disorganized, child-centred leisure was unlikely to be seen as constructive and this could have direct implications for sentencing.

Control and attitudes

A further central referent in magistrates' assessments of cases involved data which were seen to signify the *attitude* of the defendant first to the offence itself and more broadly, to authority and the rule system in general.

It's so important to get the boy or girl's attitude to the offence.

Their attitude – how they relate to authority.

Magistrates used the term 'attitude' in a variety of contexts in their accounts of information-building activities. Most centrally, attitudes were assessed as a willingness to reform (or not); genuine contrition (or not); and willingness to cooperate in punishment and control enterprise (or not).

You have to have the child's view of the offence. How they see it. How the child feels that his future is mapped out, how his life is going to be lived.

I think its important that whoever reports gets right into the character of the child, and tells us something about the child, and his attitudes towards life.

Attitudes, to me, is perhaps the single most important word I could use.

Attitude to work or school tells you an awful lot . . . attitude to life . . . it all paints the picture of the child you're trying to know.

Attitude to authority, especially at school. And his attitude to the offence – why did he do it, and what kind of punishment does he think is right.

The whole aspect of the juvenile's attitude to life is important, whether they regret the offence, if there is genuine remorse; whether they are a hard bitten criminal or if it is an offence of high spirits; because you are trying to understand if it is a crime or if it is foolish behaviour, whether they have a criminal mind or whether they are getting into scrapes.

Attitude was thus likely to be fundamental in magistrates' assessments as to whether 'something could be done' with a child or whether he or she was a 'hard case'. The key concepts for justices were 'remorse' and 'responsiveness'. A 'don't care' attitude to authority and an overt statement in the report that 'x appears to have little regret for this offence' were regarded as important negative control indicators. Incorrigibility was often viewed as worse than the offence itself.

Control and 'the criminal culture'

Magistrates exhibited a definite notion of a criminal culture which they sought to identify, partly from their own background knowledge and partly from the social inquiry report. This notion had a triple referent. It related to family, to friends and associates and to neighbourhood. It was common for offenders to be seen as existing in a network of sub-legal family activities being socialized into anti-social values.

Thus the involvement of the rest of the family in delinquency was seen as an important control indicator because it had implications for the likelihood of the family cooperating with the court in disciplining the offender and instilling into the child the 'appropriate' sentiments of remorse and regret, or alternatively the likelihood of the child's anti-social behaviour traits being condemned or reinforced:

You want to know what support is the rest of the family, how involved the rest of the family are in offending, how they are going to view the offending.

If they grow up in that kind of atmosphere they learn from those patterns.

A child brought up with elder brothers who are in trouble is more at risk. At a school where I taught, we had six brothers through, now one is in prison, and they're all at risk.

Its important to know if [offending] is a way of life in the family – if they're all like that.

The concept of family influences linked with the peer network and the neighbourhood:

It would be helpful to know whether there are brothers and sisters in trouble, although one can look at the address and know – one can form . . . an image. You can sometimes go wrong, even [x] Road has respectable families in it, so it is essential to have these details in the report.

It's the social background you are looking for – to put specifically the area where they live in [SIR], and, you know, to put comments on this area . . . because the influence is so great and . . . it's as if the council puts all these people into one area.

Often it's the company they keep, if you can get to know that – younger children hanging around with older ones who are perhaps known . . .

You often find that they are associating with a certain group.

Linked strongly in with magistrates' background knowledge of delinquent areas and 'bad schools', justices would seek information in respect of 'awful enclosures', and associated with this were strong conceptions of the delinquent family, friends and associates. Such was the strength of magistrates' beliefs about the influence of delinquent cultures that they felt it necessary to look for 'special' reasons for offending where the background seemed to be good:

If there are four children and only one is offending, you look for a particular cause.

Sometimes you get a bad apple, perhaps it's a throwback in the genes when the rest of the family are respectable and hardworking and industrious . . .

If you find a child from a good background offending then you feel that something more serious may be wrong.

Magistrates continually illustrated their accounts of the relevance of social background representations with examples of their incorporation into the sentencing process. Positive indicators suggested a down tariff influence, while negative indicators involved up tariff pressure. Thus, for example, an 'unstable' family background suggests a higher degree of intervention:

> The mother clearly couldn't discipline him. We were able to inject some of that from the outside via an AC order. You want to know the support they are receiving at home. Many are from one parent families and it affects how they behave, their mothers can't handle them. So then you try to get a disposal such as supervision and IT to help.

> If all the members of the family are delinquent, often a parental failure has occurred. It may be better to remove them from that environment.

> How you think the parents will help will affect what happens. How much control is there? Can they actually get them to comply with an order such as CSO [community service order]?

> If there is some sign that the father will take steps, curtail his freedom perhaps, then we are less likely to intervene.

> We are more likely to impose a fine if we think it will be made a punishment to [the child].

Negative familial indicators of 'indiscipline' and 'instability' generally act to push the offender up tariff towards higher degrees of intervention and the imposition of structure and surveillance from outside. When the family fails (or appears to fail) in this, then supervision orders or attendance centre orders are frequently seen to be the 'solution'. If the negative indicators are further compounded by a disinclination on the part of social services to have any involvement with the case, then the movement is further up tariff:

> They're very good at giving you the feeling as to whether somebody could work with this family or they couldn't work with this family . . . or even if they don't actually say so you can get the feeling that they're so far out on a limb that they're a bit baffled . . . and then a supervision order probably wouldn't be suitable anyway.

Through these mechanisms children with a history of care are often perceived as already up tariff by magistrates, because the 'family situation' is, by definition, unstable, and social services intervention has, by definition, 'failed'. There is then little left beyond allowing the care order to continue or a move towards attendance centre and custody orders.

Again, other negative indicators such as 'offending among other family members' or a 'lack of structured leisure time', acted as up tariff indicators:

> If all his brothers are in trouble, then it may well be better to remove them from their influence.

> If you know they're active, have constructive interests, then its something you can latch on to.

> Something to build on, perhaps through supervision and IT. If they're just wandering around, getting into trouble, then again IT might help, depending on how the family might support it.

The possession of a 'real' job could be a strong 'positive' indicator:

> They were due for DC, really, this morning. But we didn't do it because they'd got jobs. Sending them away would have wrecked their jobs, just made them resentful against the system, whereas a fine we thought would be a constant reminder to them that they'd committed a crime without taking away that basis for them making good.

Similarly, attitudes provoked positive/negative influences:

> You need to know if he has learned his lesson. I have given a lenient sentence in the full knowledge that his appearance in court on that day would be all that that child needed.

Magistrates placed continual stress on picture building as the means by which social information was operationalized in relation to the tariff. This reflected the way in which, through the interaction of the court hearing, the reading of social data and the negotiations of the retiring room, the formulation of a decision was continually intertwined with images of controllability. Pure mitigation, however, did appear to occupy a different role from control indicators, in that an 'appalling' family situation might on occasion be construed as implying a lack of culpability on the part of the child and so hold the defendant down tariff:

> Sometimes when you see the family background, you think, well, the poor kid hasn't had a chance really, from the start.

> There are the ones whose lives are a complete mess, their parents have split up, there's constant friction, they're rebelling totally against anything the parents do . . . they're the ones who probation and social services can help.

To a large extent, whether a 'bad' family background is seen as a mitigating factor or a negative control indicator will depend on the other components of the picture, the prevalence of other negative indicators, and the perceived nature of the offence itself.

This again relates to magistrates' need to draw a distinction between the 'real' criminals and those for whom offending is seen to be an aberration or a 'phase', something that they might yet be 'helped out of'. Picture building is thus a continual classification process engaged in by magistrates, based chiefly on the articulation of control indicators but also influenced by classical mitigation. As an activity, picture building is constituted in and through tariff sentencing.

In general, a consideration of magistrates' use of control indicators suggests that the major task in report reading is one of quickly assessing the extent to which the defendant is within or outwith the integrating forces of adult society. SIRs can encourage justices in this assessment by providing a series of fairly free floating data. Magistrates can utilize this to sketch out for themselves the points at which defendants appear to be linked in to the organizations and institutions (school, work, the family, adult-led youth organizations) of social order. The discourse invoked by decision makers in relation to SIRs thus embodies a wide ranging theory in use of the nature of social order and social disorder. The 'law-abiding' world is the world of the gender ordered family, of authority hierarchies of the 'work ethic', of private property: of patriarchal capitalist organization and its many and varied constituents. The wider social formation is thus directly linked with the micro-processes of juvenile sentencing as it is reproduced in the discourse and routine activities of juvenile court magistrates via their reading of reports.

CHAPTER 4

From nine until four: magistrates and school reports

It has been argued convincingly both sociologically and historically that the school operates (for working-class children at least) primarily as a mode of containment and control (Young and Whitty 1977; Corrigan 1979; Muncie 1984). In many ways the court may be seen as taking up where the school fails in this respect; the court is there as the final sanction for parents who cannot get their children to attend school and at the same time acts as a repository for the 'problem children' whom the school rejects. It is within this broader context that magistrates' reading of school reports may be seen. It is, then, perhaps of little surprise that the preoccupation with potential for control which figured largely in justices' reading of SIRs, emerged in its purest form in relation to school reports. Magistrates' interest in these documents stemmed almost entirely from their desire to have a picture of how the child fitted in to the containment and control authority hierarchies of the school. School reports were thus assessed almost solely as providers as control indicators for magistrates.

This began, first and foremost, with a concern about attendance, rather than the more subtle area of discipline within school:

I look at them mainly for truancy.

Mainly I just look for the factual information – the attendance record.

Well, it does tell you when they're not there, which is the majority of the time . . . apart from attendance, they're not an awful lot of use.

Truancy was generally taken to be a negative control indicator – that is, a sign that the child was drifting, in trouble, not under control, not living within the social fabric of decent community life:

Truancy, I look at. If they are regular attenders, then that is a source of stability.

Attendance is important. A child should be spending a lot of time in school. Frankly, a lot of the ones that we get, don't. But it should be an important part of their lives.

I watch the attendance a lot. If they truant all the time then there is something clearly the matter.

Secondly, magistrates would look for data in relation to familial control indicators; the degree of involvement of the parents with the school would be assessed in terms of whether it suggested that the parents were 'supportive', 'caring', 'concerned':

They do give you a picture taken together with the SIR . . . as with the one today, we saw that . . . his mother had been in touch with the school because she was worried about him.

It tells you whether the parents co-operate, most of the time it will say, 'no parental co-operation', or 'this is a parent who has tried, but has failed'; they do give you sufficient information about the parents which is followed through in the social report. You read between the lines whether you're getting a family that cares or not.

You get the attitude of the parents, that is useful, whether they are interested in his education.

Magistrates were thus probing the links of the 'tutelary complex' (Donzelot 1980) for weaknesses, for areas of the social structure where control had loosened (Matza 1964). Non-attendance at school was the first sign of trouble; this could only be compounded by parents who failed to show appropriate concern over this 'falling away'.

Hence the third category of information stressed by justices as useful from school reports related to the 'attitude' of the child, his or her 'behaviour' in school in relation to other pupils and in relation to authority:

The class teacher's report is extremely useful, as to what sort of influence they are, on their colleagues, whether they're . . . the leader of a disruptive minority, that information I find helps me a great deal because that sets the picture.

Their attitude to their teachers, how they respond to discipline, that sort of thing is helpful.

If they are well written I find them very useful on attitude, character, relations with their peers – generally I would favour the school report [over the SIR].

They can be very good at telling you if they are disruptive or not, that sort of thing.

I would like to see similar information to what we have already been given in the SIR but in relation to the school: his attitude to school, who are his known friends and associates, is he easily led, or is he a bully . . .

I think how they react, just even how they react with other children, is quite important, you may have a child charged with say, demanding money with menaces, now it's quite important to know how the child behaves in school.

Truancy, data which magistrates construe as a 'lack of parental in-volvement' in schooling and condemnatory statements by teachers regarding a child's attitude, behaviour in class (such as 'disruptiveness', 'bullying', 'deceitful', 'indolent' etc.) acted as immediate up tariff in-dicators because they acted to situate the child outside the network of social ties and controls which would bind them in to the normative structure of society (as seen by magistrates).

The kind of data from school reports which magistrates focused on as indicators reflected the social distance between the bench and the communities they sit in judgement upon. Behaviour of juveniles thus tended to be measured up against culturally inappropriate standards which reflected the typically middle-class lifestyles of bench members. Thus behaviour which might be very typical for working-class youth, such as a degree of non-attendance at school during the last year, became taken up as abnormality and a lack of integration. A picture is constructed in the magistrate's mind of 'the truant', a marginal charac-ter seen as probably involved in all sorts of related delinquencies, a dangerous element against and outside 'respectable society' who must be curbed before it was 'too late'. 'Parental involvement' with the school – typically a middle-class phenomenon – is similarly vested with a significance in assessing parents' willingness to 'care and control'.

Because the juvenile magistrate is likely to be, or have been, an 'active parent' (for example, a PTA member, school governor, teacher or ex-teacher), parents of children coming before the court are likely to be assessed in terms of a measure of active parenthood, despite the fact that this is largely a middle-class cultural form which is rooted in meritocratic assumptions about the role of education in children's lives. Willis has shown the inappropriateness of this kind of model for working-class youth (Willis 1977) yet for magistrates the professional values of educational achievement and a view of the school as a centre of socialization into culturally integrative forms such as good citizenship are a central pivot around which other behaviours are seen to turn. If a child is out of control in school, and if parents appear to be lacking in commitment to reinforce the values of education, then the implication (for magistrates) is that the child is on the slippery slope to social disintegration. If the school cannot control him or her and the family will not assist the school in its efforts, then the child is outwith society. The school may even be viewed as a microcosm of society, so that behaviour in school can be judged to be as important as behaviour in society proper:

> The school is a microcosm of society. So how they behave in school is important in assessing how they are likely to behave in society at large.

> They have their own law and order system within a school. So it would be useful to know if they are continually in breach of that law and order system, not necessarily 'criminal', but committing offences within that system.

In theory this indicates that a great deal of emphasis could be placed on school reports in classifying children. In practice, magistrates' orientation towards school reports was less simple than this. For despite a strong attachment in principle to the value of school reports, magistrates expressed reservations about the utility of the data:

> They ought to be useful, they ought to be very useful, because a teacher sees them all day, sees all aspects of their behaviour – in practice, they aren't, very.

This surprising ambiguity about reports emanating from an institution regarding whose value magistrates were anything but ambiguous was found to have two sources. First, as Asquith noted (Asquith 1983), the brevity of school reports could be considered a problem.

> Absolutely useless, apart from the attendance. They just tick boxes. It's the format of things, just one word answers.

> In a word, pathetic. If you get one worthwhile sentence you're lucky . . . quickly scribbled off . . . I'm quite sure that often it's wrong.

> I always feel they're prepared by teachers who are busy, resentful, grumpy. You get one word answers and they may be very unfair.

Second, and more interestingly, magistrates were anything but blind to the potential lack of impartiality in school reports. Magistrates, perhaps precisely because they were likely to have some knowledge of the teaching profession, tended to be sceptical about the way in which reports were produced.

The majority of magistrates in all courts expressed some negative comments or reservations about school reports. Magistrates expressed a sense of frustration in that the information they felt they were wanting from school reports was unreliable because of what they perceived as the judgemental and gratuitously derogatory nature of the comments in school reports. The highly judgemental character of school reports, amounting in some cases to slander, was mentioned by many magistrates:

> I object to the language – they say things like 'vicious' – it's very judgemental.

> The teacher may have formed an opinion of a child within ten seconds of seeing him. Animosity may arise between teacher and kid, and if the report's based on that then it's based on opinion. I don't know that school reports are of any great value, full stop.

> Particularly derogatory remarks lead me to think that perhaps the child has been scapegoated . . . some comments are extremely judgemental, particularly about the appearance of the child . . . they are often very, . . . hard comments. Negative comments are made about the parents, especially their social background.

> I mean it's not particularly satisfactory to have in a school report the word 'untrustworthy' underlined and nothing else.

> I mean to what degree – . . . is it perhaps just a conception that teacher has about a child?

Several justices commented that they felt the school report was chiefly aimed at 'getting rid of troublemakers' as perceived by the teachers:

> One would like to see objectivity . . . but it's generally a case of, er, 'now we've got the little bastard at long last' . . .

> I think I've discovered that the school is more concerned with retribution than the social workers . . . they've had him for two or three years and they're fed up with him . . . I certainly have discovered that.

A minority of magistrates actually made unequivocally positive comments about school reports, although many were capable of making both positive and negative assessments. Positive comments revolved around magistrates' perception of the teacher as someone who would have a better knowledge of the child than a social worker would:

> A teacher sees the child from nine 'til four. They must have a better knowledge than a social worker who sees them for perhaps an hour.

> The school sees them five days out of the week, and sees them in every situation, . . . so they must get a better idea than the social worker who is only sitting in the house for half an hour trying to suss the situation, because we all know that if you think somebody's coming you're on your best behaviour.

Interestingly those magistrates who made only positive comments about school reports tended to base these on reasons which were mirror images of the negative comments made by other justices. Thus where the majority mentioned brevity and teacher bias as negative aspects, this minority stressed conciseness and objectivity! Vice, then, becomes virtue for these respondents:

> They are adequate for what you want to know. If they say he's 'lazy', we don't need to know the story behind his laziness.

> I feel that the teacher takes a more . . . objective view, shall we say, than the social worker . . .

Thus a minority of magistrates emphasized the 'objectivity', 'conciseness', the 'reliability' of the school reports compared with SIRs. However, the large majority made at least some negative evaluations of school reports while at the same time feeling strongly that school reports ought to be more useful than SIRs because of the more extensive contact of teachers with children compared with a social worker.

A duality and tension thus existed in magistrates' reading of school reports. They were seen to be on the one hand ideal sources of control indicators and on the other as potentially flawed. Magistrates expressed themselves even more confused when it came to comparing the social images promoted by the two reports:

> One of the things that has always bothered me is that school reports and the social inquiry reports often — are often widely divergent.

It's hard to reconcile that they're talking about the same person more often than not.

There are times when the teacher may say that he is indolent and disinterested, and the social worker may say the opposite.

The last lad we had this morning, the school report said he was idling and disruptive, and the SIR said that he was well behaved.

One of the common 'human factors' in information processing (cf. Hogarth 1971) is the desire to achieve congruence across information in order for a decision to be made. The inability to do this led magistrates to adopt strategies in order to decide which report was 'nearer to the truth'. Hence they used several techniques to resolve contradictory messages:

Somewhere in the middle is usually the truth.

You just use your judgement and commonsense.

You rely on your own information you've been able to pick out in court, you weigh up the probabilities, and you use your own commonsense.

I look at the back of the social inquiry report to see who's written it. See if you can resolve it that way.

The SIR may say, 'oh, x is well behaved and helpful' etc., and the school report will say 'he's disruptive, deceitful' etc. – then you've got to decide which is nearer the truth – I often feel that the school report must be nearer the truth.

Other justices acknowledged contradictions but did not find them to be problematic:

Sometimes they contradict each other and give completely different pictures. But you would expect that a child may be different in school and outside of school. You just have to try and decide which is the most accurate.

You would expect that a child may behave differently in different settings. There are some kids who are never going to get on in school.

The problem as perceived by many magistrates was that although they felt frustrated by the inadequacy of school reports they were strongly attached to their idea of what a school report ought to be doing in terms of providing control indicators. Thus although most justices stated that they considered school reports to be ancillary to the SIR, or that they placed 'very little weight' on school reports, it is not safe to assume that adverse control indicators from school reports would not end up being used. This problem was perceived by some justices:

> I worry about school reports. I don't know whether we should have them at all, because magistrates – my impression anyway, is that they do put a lot of weight on them . . .

It is not clear to what extent in practice it is possible to block out the influence of highly directive, highly detrimental statements from a powerful source, particularly if a bench finds itself constituted with one or more strongly pro school report justices. Moreover, given the desire to obtain an integrated picture of the defendant, it is sobering to consider how a word such as 'deceitful' or 'lazy' underlined, might be interpreted when aligned with a range of other possibly ambiguous messages (from SIRs, parents and juveniles in court, solicitors . . .).

It also seemed clear that a strong belief in the objectivity of the school report and of its value, coincided with a low value being attached to the SIR and also to some extent with a lack of commitment to a fully extended tariff. Thus the minority of justices who considered school reports to be more valuable than the SIR tended also to be those who valued the school report because it was 'tough', 'not just trying to get them off'. Relatively 'hard' benches such as A and E contained a higher proportion of justices who were unequivocally positive about school reports. Conversely, in courts B and C, the courts with the longest 'slippery slopes' and lower custody rates, school reports were much more likely to be discounted as useful sources of information.

This suggests that for magistrates with a restrictive view of the tariff, the more directly punitive line taken by the schools is preferred because it supports the existing orientation of the magistrates towards the tariff. Partly, moreover, the brevity of the school report encourages this to happen, for 'bullying' and 'anti-social attitudes' can be interpreted in any number of ways, as well as discounted on the same basis. Hence school reports occupy an uneasy place in the processing of juveniles. Magistrates tended to cope with this by using school report data highly selectively, picking out attendance figures and other limited indicators in order to achieve, if possible, a congruence with other data. The ambiguities and problems were clearly stated by one justice:

> They are always read. I mean, they are never ignored. But the usual process is to read the attendance record and see if there are

any raised eyebrows or not, then depending on the fullness of the comments made you make a judgement about the teacher – derogatory comments may produce an antipathy towards the writer.

It goes together with the SIR to form a picture.

Taken together with the SIR, it can be a help, but I would regard the SIR as the main thing.

It seems likely from magistrates' discussions of specific cases that unless the school report was regarded as completely 'over the top', then it would be accorded influence. Except in a small minority of cases, moreover, that influence would be a push out of the school gates and 'down the slope' towards custody. The process of reading school reports was thus different from the process of reading SIRs. Although justices operated a search for control indicators in a manner comparable to the way they used the SIR, that process was fraught with uncertainty. While a 'good' school report would certainly act as a down- tariff indicator (regular attendance, good academic perfor- mance, regular parent school contact, 'positive' attitude to authority), a 'bad' school report would not necessarily result in up tariff pressure (excepting a poor attendance record) unless other control indicators were seen as consistent with this or the school had resolutely refused to have anything more to do with the child. None the less, it seems fair to suggest that other conditions being favourable, the school re- port as interpreted by justices could have some very undesirable effects for the offender. This has certainly received support from recent re- search carried out by Sumner, Jarvis, and Parker (1988). Sumner *et al* found that negative school report data, where 'Educational issues often shaded into disciplinary issues' (Sumner *et al.* 1988: 15) could influ- ence the bench towards custodial dispositions – as with the boy who received a six-month youth custody disposal partly because he 'could not accept authority in the school football team' (*ibid*: 17).

Given that much of the data in such reports is unsubstantiated (and in practical terms unsubstantiable), and often 'secret' (that is, not dis- closed to offenders/parents (cf. Ball 1983), the defendant versus the school is a one-sided contest.

CHAPTER 5

Writing for an audience: magistrates' views of 'professional judgement'

As they grade us on how we deal with reports, so we grade them on the quality of their reports. The styles become familiar . . . we have a working relationship.

Magistrate, 15 years service

Any social inquiry report presented to the bench intervenes in a history. It plays a part in the interorganizational exchanges of which reports are one instance, so that there is always a context which has been partly negotiated, the sentencing ethos into which reports are received.

Agencies' awareness of this context has been demonstrated in several studies (for example, Carlen 1976; Paley and Leeves 1982; Davies 1974). Davies, for example, proposed in the following model:

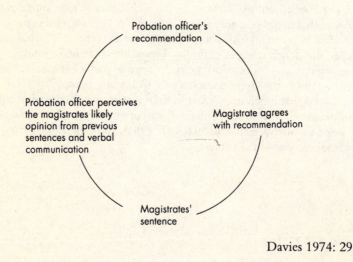

Davies 1974: 29

Davies's research was later developed by Hardiker (1975) and critically assessed by Paley and Leeves (1982). Research concentrating on the interactions of the courtroom has, moreover, stressed the negotiated, strategically achieved, nature of sentencing (Parker, Casburn and Turnbull 1981; Smith and May 1980; Carlen 1976; Cicourel 1968). Every case dealt with may thus re-create or threaten the existing 'reality' of bench–agency relationships, an always temporary formation of interlocking assumptions and expectations on the part of magistrates and report writers.

This chapter will primarily concentrate on bench–agency relationships as histories and will seek to analyse how magistrates' perceptions of the 'quality' of reports are inserted into that history.

Individual report writers and perceived quality of reports

It was sometimes found to be the case that an individual probation officer or social worker might have more or less credibility with magistrates as a 'good' officer. This would be a reputation built up over time and could develop solely through familiarity with reports produced by that writer or through a combination of exposure to reports and personal contact with the agency worker:

> I'll be honest. I think one tends to rely a great deal on the particular probation officer or the particular social worker that's done the report. Because I've learned that there are certain people who I can trust almost implicitly . . . because in the past he's [*sic*] proved to be so right.

> You get to know each other. It would be impossible not to be influenced by your knowledge of the individual officer.

> Because we know our officers – one I have known for ten years – it does affect how you look at it.

> You do know the officers in B, and to be honest you do put more credence on some than others.

In courts B and D, the smallest benches studied, and to a lesser extent in courts C and A, knowledge of individual report writers was common and generally involved informal contact, meeting through liaison committees, or through other activities outside the court, as well as past experience of the person's reports.

In courts E and F, such contacts were less frequent, being mainly limited to certain active and long serving members of the juvenile panel. In these courts, magistrates were also less likely to build up a familiarity with the signatures at the end mentioned by many justices in other courts:

> I only have to read a report to know who's written it. (B)

> I . . . always look at the back of a report first to see who's written it. (D)

> [If there is conflict between school report and SIR] I look at the end to see who's written it [SIR]. (A)

> I don't think I would recognise a particular report as being written by an *individual* . . . (E)

Where individuals *are* known personally to magistrates (or where they are known through their report writing), then magistrates made a clear association between individuals and quality of reports. The sense in which this was not just a question of individual magistrates' perceptions, but also a matter of bench history, is illustrated nicely:

> I don't because I'm new to the bench, but other magistrates say, 'oh, yes, if so-and-so's written it it's bound to be good', or 'oh, don't take any notice of that, so-and-so's written it. It's like anything else, individuals tend to build up a reputation. (D)

Can individual report writers 'make history'?

Carlen in *Magistrates' Justice* cites a probation officer as saying:

> If you start soft-pedalling with those whom the magistrate feels, and society feels, shouldn't be soft-pedalled with, then, when you have a genuine recommendation going against the grain, then it wouldn't be accepted.
>
> cited in Carlen 1976: 62

This may be compared with a comment made by one of the magistrates in the present study:

> You think right, well, Mrs [ ] is a jolly good social worker, so if this is what she thinks then perhaps I ought to think about it more carefully before I decide what to do . . . we might think, well, she's very experienced, she's always given us very good reports, let's think about this again . . . (C)

In one sense a perceived need by individual social workers or probation officers to build credibility with the bench is understandable. It relates both to the need to be viewed as competent and to the desire to gain tactical advantages in terms of influence on sentencing. In the degree to which report writers utilize credibility building as a strategy, they reinforce a particular (and common) form of bench–agency relations. Although a 'good' officer is more likely to get an unusual recommendation accepted this is dependent upon her or his recommendations having been 'sensible' in the past and on her/his conventions of report writing falling within the limits found acceptable by justices.

Other chapters have considered in more detail what sort of data magistrates considered to be useful and the nature of the good and bad report will not be discussed here in depth. On a general level consistent criteria emerged which were employed by magistrates in reaching their assessment of an individual report writer.

First, a magistrate might build an impression of the 'realism' of writers, or conversely, their 'idealism'. This usually referred to writers of reports who consistently recommended disposals outside of magistrates' perceptions of an appropriate tariff bracket:

> Sometimes you think, well, crikey, are they grasping at straws!

> You do start looking at some individuals and saying, oh, look, it's so-and-so recommending a conditional discharge, he would say that, he always says that . . .

> You have some – often it's a new social worker – who are far too idealistic.

> We have one particular social worker . . . who recommends attendance centre every time. When that happens you just tend to push it to one side.

Particular officers could come to be labelled soft or naive while others could be designated realistic, not just trying to get them off. Magistrates in court E particularly praised one social worker who was known to recommend custody as 'willing to put their professional integrity on the line.

Second, magistrates would develop a view of a report writer as experienced (and therefore worth listening to) or not experienced (and therefore not worth listening to). Frequently the 'problem' social workers were identified as those being fresh from college who were considered to be inept at getting underneath initial appearances, likely to be hoodwinked:

> You can tell when it's a chap who's been writing reports for some time, who knows what he's really talking about. And you can sense the novice feeling his way . . .

You get to know officers . . . you judge when they become more mature by the depth of their report and their realism – sometimes it's obvious they are being hoodwinked by a notorious family; and some always insist on recommending a particular thing.

Third, magistrates contrasted those report writers who were known to promote 'theories' or 'political views' with those who could be relied upon to display 'commonsense'. Examples of the former given by magistrates included social workers who used the ineffectiveness of custody as an argument for a non-custodial sentence or material deprivation/unemployment as an explanation for offending. This was related to the style in which such arguments were expressed for, as 'theory' was seen to be related to 'idealism', so 'commonsense' was linked to 'plain English'. Report writers were expected to follow the conventions of report writing in providing a narrative-style, pathologically centred document which concurred with the search for control indicators and mitigating factors, focusing on the individual and expressed in a language of 'commonsense'.

A circularity is thus established in that a continual tactical awareness on the part of report writers as to what magistrates will and will not 'wear' reinforces magistrates' expectations of reports. A minimal and occasional gain in terms of getting an unusual recommendation through is made at the expense of longer-term conformity. Any individual who then breaks the tacit agreement will either be discounted by justices – their reports 'pushed to one side' – or disciplined, as was the case at court E where the chair of the juvenile panel complained through the court officer about an individual's 'way out' recommendations. The end result of credibility building by report writers leads to a fine line between gaining the respect of the bench and simply reinforcing the sentencing practice and interpretive conventions of the bench.

Any change in report writing practice, or any challenge to magistrates' assumptions, is therefore unlikely to be successful at an individual level whilst the collective practice of agencies reinforces the status quo. 'There can be a problem with new social workers. But they usually come round to our way of thinking' (D).

Agencies and the perceived value of reports

It has been seen that individual report writers were unlikely to be able to exert influence by a personal change in report writing practice. Individuals were far more effective in re-creating already existing history than they could be in trying to alter its course. A reputation as a trusted social worker or probation officer provides little scope for innovations in dealing with juvenile cases. Moreover, magistrates at larger courts were unlikely to form impressions of individual report writers.

At the collective level of the agency magistrates were more likely to make a strong link between perceptions of the quality of reports and perceptions of the value of the agency. There was also more potential to exert an impact on magistrates' handling of juvenile cases at agency level. Magistrates' evaluations of reports (collectively) influenced their views of the agency and in turn the regard in which they held the agency affected the influence which they accorded reports (collectively). 'I think that the fact that we trust the *service* is important . . . I accept that [the report] is a product of the service that's come before me.'

Magistrates' perceptions of the quality of relationships between bench and agencies may derive from an accretion of perceptions of reports actually provided over time, from magistrates' encounters with agency representatives in liaison activities and, less directly, from magistrates' general attitude towards the value of probation or social work in dealing with 'juvenile crime'. These sources are themselves interactive so that clearly magistrates with a more positive perception of social work are more likely to take part in liaison activities or, in other cases, an almost accidental participation in liaison activities may result in a more positive perception of probation/social work.

> I used to be much more suspicious of them before I went on the liaison committee. I didn't think they should make recommendations . . . but now I think it's alright.

The first line of magistrates' general perceptions of agencies clearly stemmed from their experience of report provision over time. Magistrates' most regular contact with agencies comes through the reports. Judgements such as left wing, idealist, professional people trying to do their best, on the side of the defendant and so on, were very often made about agencies by reading off images from social inquiry reports. Again, however, a feedback loop exists because a negative orientation towards social work could clearly affect the receptivity of justices to individual reports: 'The juvenile justice system worked perfectly well without [social workers] prying into peoples' lives . . . I don't take any notice of SIRs.' This strength of feeling, however, tended to occur at the level of the idiosyncratic, where a magistrate with particularly rigid beliefs maintained a position outside the broadly collective culture of the interpretive conventions articulated by the majority of her or his colleagues.

Because magistrates' always already existing interpretive frameworks strongly govern the way in which they create information from report data, the importance of liaison activities is underlined for agencies wishing to affect the way in which juvenile cases are handled. While in the long term expectations of reports may be changed through a change in report-writing policy at agency level, any more fundamental change must entail some deeper penetration into the perceptual conventions of justices – into the way in which magistrates read. Ironically, the agencies themselves have actively helped to create expectations of pathologically centred documents amenable to the search for control indicators (see Chapter 2). Change then requires much more momentum *because* this history of expectations has been created. A simple change in report-writing practice would almost certainly cause conflict and hostility unless the broader question of existing expectations and interpretive conventions is tackled first.

The crux of the receptivity of magistrates to agency influence lies in the ability or otherwise of an agency to enrol the bench (or key members of it) into broad acceptance of a general strategy in processing juvenile cases. This may be illustrated with reference to two contrasting histories of bench–agency relations: those of court E and court B.

As an *agency*, the social services department in court E made very little impact on the bench:

> We used to have formal meetings but they were a waste of time. We have had talks and lectures . . . but there is no grassroots interaction to speak of.

> You don't get to know social workers. It's less man-to-man than it was [i.e. during the 'probation era'].

For E magistrates, 'relationships' referred to in court transactions with the court officer and the ability to communicate discontent with 'poor' reports back to the report writers via the court officer – although in practice this tended to occur only where recommendations were 'way out':

> This morning the clerk said she thought the reports were 'surfacey', and I thought they were, but I won't do anything about it and I don't suppose she will either . . .

Occasional talks and presentations were mentioned in passing without any great degree of enthusiasm by magistrates:

Social services may come and present a talk . . . they did quite a bit of research on ways in which we dealt with people compared with national trends . . . very interesting, but whether it's cost effective, I don't know . . .

Professor X came to talk to us – I think he must make quite a lot of money giving talks because we paid him £150 and he gave talks at [other courts] as well. Anyway, he told us a lot of statistics about how there wouldn't be many juveniles in 10 years time so juvenile crime would reduce . . . so I asked him, what would he do with the persistent house burglar . . . he couldn't answer . . .

Magistrates at court E, with a few exceptions, showed little interest in deepening their involvement with the social services department. The tenor of relationships was bench led, with little positive intervention from agencies. Report writers would from time to time recommend custody (see Chapter 2) and win magistrates' approval for 'realism'; the court officer played his court and made occasional strategic gains. Wider interaction was limited to guest speakers at formal liaison meetings and the occasional visits to social services establishments.

The topography of bench–agency relations in court B presents a contrast to that of E. A much smaller juvenile panel than court E's (18 magistrates compared with 39), with the juvenile court sitting only twice a month, meant that magistrates knew each other and the agencies better than at court E, with the volume of cases to process also being much lower. Agency provision also differed: in court B, probation and social services both dealt with juvenile cases. Probation SIRs were all prepared by one probation officer who also presented the reports in court; and justices were more likely to know social workers individually either through their appearance in court for their cases (fairly routine at B but unusual at E) or through liaison activities. A close liaison existed between the probation officer and the leader of the local intensive intermediate treatment programme, who in turn had a particularly good relationship with the chair of the juvenile panel.

These kind of organizational linkages outside the boundary of the court itself, virtually absent in court E, led to a fairly tight knit relationship between court and agencies:

We have an advantage over other courts in that being small, we can build up working relationships – then we have the strength and the ability to change things – and we do have that in B.

We do attend liaison meetings. But we also have personal contacts in the agencies, and the Chairman is very good at fostering
this . . . [the leader] of [IIT project] is very helpful – he has made
a big effort to get closely involved with the bench. And the
more that happens, the more information they provide us with,
and the more effect it has.

Such linkages, as this magistrate suggested, were actively promoted by
agencies as well as panel members:

We have deliberately sought to create a strong relationship in B.
I feel that I know most of the magistrates and they know me.

Probation officer, B

I like to regard it as an educative process. That's the key – we're
trying to educate the bench. I send them progress reports on all
the kids, and I ring them up and ask them round. I try and make
sure that as many as possible get involved.

Leader, IIT project

A stronger reciprocal relationship existed between B magistrates
and agencies than at court E, partly due to the initiative of agencies
themselves and partly stemming from conditions favourable to that
initiative. Apart from the smallness of the B juvenile court, an ideological climate appeared to exist which was conducive to the development of non-custodial and low intervention approaches to
juvenile offending. The chair of the juvenile panel took a loosely anti-
custodial view of juvenile sentencing. The composition of the panel
tended more towards an enlightened liberalism (as far as the indirect
evidence of bench politics allows of such an interpretation).

While it is difficult to draw more than tentative conclusions from
the limited amount of data collected on complex histories, it seems
that contrasting bench–agency relationships have played at least some
part in producing very different sentencing profiles for courts E and B.
Court B was the only court from the six areas studied which did not
display a tariff profile, with a much higher commitment to discharge
and fines and virtually no custody rate (again care must be taken given
the low throughput of cases – see Appendix 2).

Probation and social services: magistrates' differential perceptions of agencies

The weak link in all courts, even in court B, was perceived by several
magistrates to be the relationship of the bench with social services

departments. While E magistrates (or at any rate, the longer serving ones) hankered back to the days of probation reports, magistrates in the other five court areas spoke of their better relationship with the probation service:

> There is a feeling that there may be more confidence in the probation service. There's not quite the same confidence in social services – you tend to feel they're leaning over backwards on the side off the defendant rather than balancing the offence and the offender. (D)

> Sometimes social workers . . . not being officers of the court themselves, seem to have, not to have their heart in the process the court is participating in, whereas probation are used to working in the courts and it shows . . . I think that probation officers are that little bit more realistic. (F)

> Social services, I don't seem to be able to relate to them whatsoever. I find it very difficult to agree with anything they do. Probation I've got an awful lot more sympathy for . . . I feel I've got a much better relationship with probation. There seem to be so many of them [i.e. social workers] whereas probation is fairly small and with the routine meetings we have, you get to know the probation officers . . . (A)

> We have regular meetings with probation officers, we get to know each other . . . liaison with social services, we haven't had many meetings the last year or two, I haven't been to a meeting with them for the last couple of years. (C)

> We don't have so much contact with social services, whereas all of us can have close contact with the probation service. That's the good thing about the probation service – you do *know* the probation officer. Whereas social services – well, I've never had any contact with them. (B)

Magistrates commented upon the lack of opportunity to meet social workers, the lack of expertise of social workers in the 'rules of the game' in court and the approach taken by social workers to report writing, which was claimed to be more theoretical, 'jargon-bound' and idealistic. Probation SIRs, in contrast, were said to be better argued, more 'factual', 'realistic' and more grounded in 'common-sense' and 'experience'. Magistrates' feelings about a lack of strong relationships with social services were thus reflected in their evaluations of SIRs provided by social workers, as the following categories suggest.

- Realism versus Idealism:

  Sometimes with the social workers, they're a little bit airy-fairy, you can see they're straight out of university and they've got this wonderful idealistic way . . .

  I prefer a probation report any time. They are more realistic – social workers' reports are airy-fairy, full of jargon. (D)

  Probation reports are more realistic in their recommendations, social workers give an impression of being more client-oriented, they don't take into account the wider aspects. (F)

  The probation service tend to be more realistic . . . (C)

- Style and 'factual' content:

  Social services tend to be more . . . diffuse, whereas probation reports are more trimmed. (B)

  Social workers tend to write to a pattern, and probation reports are more clearly done, presenting the most essential information in detail. (B)

  Social workers' SIRs read as if they have been dictated. They are far too verbose . . . they're very subjective and there's a lot of 'chat'. (C)

- Experience:

  We have got a fairly 'old' probation team, some of them have been here for ten or fifteen years, and it does show in their reports. Experience is very important. (D)

  Probation reports are prepared by someone more experienced and it does show through. (B)

- Professionalism:

  I do think that probation officers tend to be a little bit more professional, really. (A)

  Probation is a more . . . professional service. (D)

Thus while some magistrates referred to the inferior language and style of social workers' reports, others criticized what they perceived as a tendency to idealism. This, it was felt, tended to stem as much from lack of experience as from the nature of the service. Magistrates referred to social workers' tendencies 'always to recommend discharges' (an impression which appeared to stem partially from the fact that social workers prepared reports on offenders who were already in care and had no income, leaving little else to recommend).

Overall the majority of magistrates' comments about social workers' reports may be seen as relating to social workers' lack of fit with the court regime, in turn a product of the different relationship of the two agencies to the juvenile court system. Ultimately, social workers were seen to lack *tactical* sense:

> I think it's that probation officers are more used to being in court, more used to presenting their reports to a court . . . so they tend to write reports in very straight-forward English which any magistrate can comprehend. Now . . . the social worker thinks in terms of his own training, knows all the little words and phrases which are used in this science, but doesn't go to court a lot, doesn't often appreciate that the court won't understand, or will *dislike* the expressions. Sometimes social workers, not being officers of the court themselves, seem to have . . . not to have their heart in the process the court is participating in, whereas probation are used to working in the courts and it shows in the attitude and the sort of suggestions made . . . probation officers are that little bit more realistic . . . the reports have a *tactical* function . . . I think there's a lot of – there's an art, an *art* to doing a probation report . . . (F)

> They should have sufficient experience to have a pretty fair idea of what's going to happen. Be a bit practical about it. And then, if they think the youngster's worth it, try and pull them back from the edge . . . it may be that they think that they are trying to be more helpful by giving us as comprehensive a report as possible . . . some do seem to waffle and it doesn't always seem relevant. Particularly if they've formed a good relationship. (C)

The main focus here is on the *reasons* for some magistrates' (around one-third of the total interviewed in courts A,B,C,D and F, probation reports not being provided on juvenile cases in court E) preference of probation SIRs, and for perceptions of a better relationship with the probation service. These very much relate to a perception on the part of magistrates that probation officers are servants of the court, part of the system, who know better, and play within, organizational conventions. As an agency, therefore, the probation service – just as individuals skilled in strategy – are more likely to be able to make limited gains with their reports in pulling individuals 'back from the edge'. Realism thus essentially refers to an appreciation of, and acquiescence in, the tariff bracket within which magistrates are likely to work in a particular case.

Can agencies make history?

In one sense agencies at the collective level have the potential to adopt effective strategies through their working relationship with magistrates. Whereas an individual report writer may 'pull one back from the brink' by taking a careful approach to the style of her/his reports and pattern of recommendations, an agency may be in a position to coopt key members of the bench into, for example, low intervention approaches to juvenile sentencing. To some extent this had occurred in court B, as far as can be ascertained from limited evidence.

Ultimately, however, there is an asymmetry of power between agencies and magistrates which is inherent in the need for agencies to influence the bench. In making history, therefore, agencies always need to be perceived as within the bounds of existing conventions: they must be seen as experienced, realistic and grounded in commonsense with all the connotations which that carries for interpreting juvenile offending. Nor should it be assumed that agencies necessarily wish to change bench practices: many may share very similar goals in processing juvenile cases as the magistrates themselves, similarly classifying 'soft end', 'intermediate' and 'hard core' cases in relation to familial pathology.

The greatest asymmetry of power is between all the processors, whether bench or agency, and the children who become the objects of juvenile justice. While bench–agency strategies may produce important differences in outcomes for some juveniles (lesser or greater likelihood of receiving custodial sentences, for example), the overall nature of juvenile processing was characterized more by its generality over ostensibly different benches, than by conflict. Little evidence was found in any area of a successful challenging of the interpretive conventions of magistrates in dealing with juvenile cases. Even in court B, the agencies' success may be attributable more to the small size of the bench and its low caseload, enabling a strong clerk and chair (sharing liberal ideologies) to dominate the sentencing ethos. Magistrates' perceptions of the relevance of social information, of offenders and of the nature and pathology of juvenile crime, differed little at court B from other benches. It is these perceptual conventions which are both symptomatic and constitutive of the fundamental inequalities in the juvenile court system, many of which have not yet come to be regarded as problematic by magistrates or, just as importantly, by *agencies*.

Macmillan's observation of juvenile liaison panels in action, for example, suggests that in many cases, welfare professionals actually utilize interpretive conventions similar to those of the magistrates discussed in the present study (personal communication from J. Mac-millan 1989). While this is beyond the scope of the present discussion, it does suggest the dangers of assuming that agencies *would wish* to fundamentally alter the nature of juvenile justice. To a certain extent it may be suggested that agencies too are locked into the routine prac-tices of the organization of juvenile justice, so that (whether con-sciously intentional or not) the bench–agency relationship is characterized by collusion rather than conflict. The localized dis-courses of the juvenile system thus furnish a body of knowledge which acts as a technique of power in the depiction and disposition of the 'good, the bad, and the ugly' (cf. Parker 1981).

CHAPTER 6

Juveniles, parents, magistrates

This chapter considers the way in which magistrates actively manufacture information not from documents but from juvenile offenders and their parents themselves. It also considers, using observation data, the structure and content of exchanges between magistrates, parents and defendants, and considers the generation and deployment of information representations through those exchanges. Initially, magistrates interviewed claimed to gain little or no information directly from defendants or their parents: 'They have very little to say. Usually they are overawed.'

What did become apparent, however, was that despite this lack of overt communication, magistrates *were* gaining information from defendants and parents, in a rather different way:

> You look at them for character and reliability and you can assess them at a moment's notice. Then it's up to the defence and the SIR to try and get 'em off.

Similarly, another magistrate commented: 'You can tell, sometimes, its their demeanour, their general character, more than what they actually say.' Thus, while on one level magistrates were quite prepared to admit that they were presented with little of the 'real' defendant in the courtroom situation, they continued an active search for data which could be brought into the picture-building process.

It became clear that magistrates were looking for different kinds of clues from the appearance and presentation of self of parents and defendants. These could be categorized as follows:

1 moral character of parents/guardians (= 'decency');

2 evidence of an affective bond between parents or guardians and offender;
3 ability of parent/s or guardian/s to control their offspring;
4 attitude of defendant to the offence, to the courtroom situation and particularly to magistrates themselves;
5 'character' of defendant.

Thus in relation to the first category, one magistrate commented:

> From the appearance of the parent . . . you get some idea of . . . what sort of sentence you should impose, because if you think they're decent parents . . . then that's going to make all the difference, isn't it?

Magistrates also look for evidence of affective relationships, particularly for the 'caring' mother. This was apparently seen in terms of a willingness on the part of a mother to participate in the decision of the court: 'Just looking at that mother this morning you could see that she was caring, anxious about her son, that she really wanted to help.'

The 'caring' mother was not a positive indicator, however, where caring was defined as indulgent, over-protective or some kind of purely emotional bond by justices. It was clear that magistrates' sympathy for the plight of the mother might have an input into the sentencing process in more than one direction:

> Your heart warms to those poor women. Whether that has an ameliorative effect on the sentence or not I'm not quite sure . . .

Similarly mothers were often cited as unreliable sources of information since they were obviously likely to be over-protective:

> I mean, that woman this morning. She was obviously just shielding her son. Its natural and understandable, but it meant you couldn't put any reliance on what she said.

There was a clear gender effect in the reading of visual data by magistrates. Justices were essentially looking for a conformity to the strong image of the 'basically decent family'. This is consistent with their reading of social data in general (see Chapters 2 and 3). Magistrates placed great emphasis on finding evidence of the 'good' mother and the 'strong father figure'. The gender constituted family operates centrally throughout justices' readings as an indicator of the ability of the family to discipline youth and therefore as an effective part of youth control as a larger enterprise. Mothers alone, however, were clearly regarded as somewhat unstable. They were liable to be categorized as over-protective/indulgent or as indifferent or morally disreputable. Being caring was rarely enough by itself, without the input of the father figure (who would be viewed as more likely to provide the necessary discipline and structure). In this sense the appearance of both parents at the court hearing – particularly where they were regarded as the defentant's 'real parents' (i.e. not step parents or cohabitees) was seen to be a positive control indicator.

> I like to see both parents in court, not just the mother. That is an influence in itself.

> Particularly if you get both parents in court . . . you can get an idea as to whether they can handle him.

Thirdly, magistrates clearly sought 'information' in the court situation about the ability of parents or guardians to control the juvenile. Several justices stated that it was easy to tell whether the parents were likely to be able to 'help' or whether they were at the end of their tether. One magistrate stated the problem as he perceived it with some clarity:

> Nine times out of ten, they're not capable of expressing themselves . . . [or] they're sick and tired of the whole bloody thing anyway . . . one remembers with interest if one has got an articulate parent who can help, and it's the exception rather than the rule by a long chalk.

Part of the picture for magistrates was also their view of how the child appeared to conduct her/himself in court. This was chiefly a matter of sifting out the 'hard cases':

> Some of them won't make eyeball to eyeball contact . . . I've experienced looking at somebody and getting a very hard, aggressive glare back.

'The way he looked at us' could often be invoked as a contributory factor to an up tariff penalty, being seen as indicative of a lack of respect for authority and more especially as threatening the self-perceived authority of the bench. Perhaps even more vaguely, magistrates searched the demeanour of the offender for 'character':

> You can tell a lot just from their . . . demeanour, really, whether they are really hardened or whether they are frightened.

Overall, magistrates were looking for some sign of malleability and deference rather than a conventional appearance, about which they tended to be quite cynical, often referring to defendants as being washed, brushed and briefed by their social worker or defence solicitor before coming to court. It is social cohesion above all which concerns magistrates, particularly the role of the family as the necessary cornerstone for law and order:

> If you have the boy or girl in front of you, you know you get a feeling . . . I think a lot of lady magistrates, you do a lot of things by . . . yes, your intuition, you can get an idea, if the parents come to court, you can get a feeling, there's enough between the parent and the kid . . . you get some very macho men, and they'll handle a situation.

Implicit in the information search of magistrates in the court situation is the striving to identify the potentially decent family which mirrors their approach to social inquiry reports. For the majority of magistrates, information search is related to a classification of the 'decent' and the 'hopeless case', the inherently 'criminal' and the victim of circumstance.

While magistrates lamented the inarticulacy of offenders and their parents, it was clear from the observation sessions that juveniles and parents were *silenced* in court (cf. Carlen 1976; McBarnet 1981). Analysis of the observation data suggests that offenders were treated as potentially 'unruly resources' (cf. Law 1986) in a court setting. It appeared that these unruly resources had to be managed firmly in the few dialogues which they were permitted to enter into at all. The range of acceptable responses to questions was narrowly defined and controlled, with the result that much of the proceedings appeared to be somewhat bemusing for many defendants and their families:

> *Chair.* What have you got to say about this, Shaun?
> *Shaun:* (Silence – one minute)
> *Chair.* (Impatiently) Stand up Shaun, and speak to the magistrates. Tell them about the offence, your view of it, what do you think about it?
> *Shaun:* (Silence 30 seconds. Hesitantly) . . . You mean, why I did it?
> *Chair.* (Peremptorily) Yes! Why you did it, whether you regret doing it. You've stolen things before, haven't you?
> *Shaun:* Ah . . . er . . . I regret doing it.
> *Chair.* Why? Because you got caught or because it's wrong?
> *Shaun:* Because it's wrong.
> *Chair.* Why did you do it?
> *Shaun:* (Silence for some two minutes, then, almost inaudibly) It was just there.
> *Chair.* So, you've been in court before for stealing things and

you just took it because it was there even though you knew it was wrong?

Shaun: Yes.

Chair: Have you got any interests in life, what do you do apart from hanging around with your friends?

Shaun: (Silence 30 seconds) I go scrambling.

Chair: Where do you do that?

Shaun: Up at [ ].

Chair: Do you have your own bike?

Shaun: No.

Chair: Are you good at it?

Shaun: Alright.

Chair: 'Alright'. (Sighs audibly. Pause) When do you do it? In the evenings, at weekends? After school?

Shaun: After school.

Chair: Don't you think that's a better thing to be doing than hanging round with your friends, getting into trouble, stealing things? There are a lot of people trying to help you, yes . . . (half to self) there are problems (looks down at reports).

Shaun: Yes.

Chair: Sit down Shaun. Mrs Corrigan . . .

Recalling Law's definition of translation as a process of 'articulating conceptions of the world and the roles of actors that are in it and imposing those conceptions on another', it can be seen that the chair expends a good deal of energy in attempting to enrol Shaun into his project of translating the individual into a categorizable entity which may be comprehended in a language of control indicators: intentionality, remorse, commitment to a moral order expressing respect for private property, appropriate and inappropriate 'integrative' and 'disintegrative' leisure activities. Shaun, unable to reply easily in the appropriate terms (i.e. those terms implicitly held to be appropriate by the chair) hangs silent and somewhat confounded for most of the exchange. He offers a resistance to enrolment despite himself, except when he is able to correctly identify the cues for response in the magistrate's tone or words.

Most defendants appeared to be sensitive to the demand for enrolment and if pressed into more than the briefest exchanges with magistrates would attempt to offer utterances in compliance with this. Frequently, however, defendants found the terms of enrolment hopelessly unfathomable. In the case cited above, Shaun clearly perceived that 'it was just there' would not be considered an appropriate response to the question of motive and was hesitant and unwilling in giving this response; but when pressed, was unable to do 'better'. The chair in turn was unable to respond to such a reply and changed completely towards another area of control indicators. Shaun had been quite able to pick up the clue that his behaviour had been 'wrong', but the question of motive had proved too difficult. In the end, he managed a patchy contribution to the enrolment process, helped along by the strong directiveness of the magistrate, for example in the questions on 'because you got caught, or because it's wrong', and 'don't you think that's a better thing to be doing than' . . .

The question of motive continually recurred as problematic in magistrates' attempts to enrol defendants. It was almost inevitably the first or second question which the chair asked of a defendant and the one which a defendant was least able to answer in an appropriate manner. Whatever answer could be given would almost certainly be unacceptable and most defendants either stayed silent or replied that they did not know. This was certainly the safest response from their point of view for any attempt to provide a realistic account of motive would almost certainly provoke an adverse reaction from the bench. 'We was just bored' or 'we did it for a laugh' or 'it just happened' created severe conflict.

Lack of resistance to enrolment (that is, compliance) was clearly stressed as important to defendants by their parents, social workers and defence solicitors:

> Now when the magistrates come back, stand up straight and look at them, look as if you are paying attention to what they say. You don't want them to think you don't care.

Or again:

> *Chair:* What have you got to say about this offence, Ian?
> *Ian:* Uhm . . . (silence)
> *Ian's mother:* Well, say you're sorry then!
> *Ian:* I'm sorry.

Parents with some grasp of the 'rules of the game' (cf. Carlen 1976) would thus attempt to encourage their offspring into compliance. But often they were almost as lost as the juveniles themselves. They could also prove just as unruly in resisting compliance – as indeed, with Shaun's mother, who was perhaps less concerned than Ian's to 'say the right thing':

> *Chair:* Mrs Corrigan (Shaun's mother), what do you think about all this?
> *Mrs Corrigan:* Well. (sighs loudly) I don't know. He's a problem.

It is difficult. He just doesn't take any notice. He goes out all the time.

Chair: Where does he go?

Mrs Corrigan: I don't know.

Chair: Why don't you keep him at home more?

Mrs Corrigan: (Defensively) Well. We've tried. We got a video because we hoped he would stop in more and watch it, but he didn't.

Chair: (Increasingly disapprovingly) What time does he come in, does he have a set time?

Mrs Corrigan: (Long silence) Well . . . about nine, weekdays. But he comes in and just sits there. Won't tell us anything. (Pause) – he has been staying in and watching the video these last couple of weeks.

Chair: I expect that was because he knew he was coming here. What about his school attendance, do you try and make sure that he gets to school? (adopts sharply admonitory tone) His school attendance is *appalling*! 41, 51 out of 100. There have been a *lot* of people trying to help him, 1, 2, (counts from SIR) *9* people, Mrs Corrigan!

Mrs Corrigan: (Extremely defensively) Well I can't make him can I? He won't walk with his mam, he'd say all the other kids were laughing at him. He's grown up.

Chair: He's *14*, Mrs Corrigan!

Mrs Corrigan: I *know*!

Chair: In fact he doesn't seem to relate very well to the family at all, does he? Very well, the bench will retire.

Later, in discussing the issue of costs, this case got even more out of hand. Mrs Corrigan had protested at having to pay ten pounds prosecution costs, suggesting that it be paid at a pound a week by her son:

Chair: Can't you pay it yourself within 28 days? After all, you've got quite a reasonable income coming into the home.

Mrs Corrigan: Well no, not really, no. I haven't. I've to pay my gas and my electricity myself, that's £28 a week, then there's the video to be paid for.

Chair: Well, this is more important than the video, Mrs Corrigan.

Mrs Corrigan: [Defiantly] Well I've got it now, haven't I? I can't send it back, can I?

Chair: I'm *sorry* Mrs Corrigan, but court dues must come first!

We will give you 28 days to pay. Shaun, Mrs Corrigan, you
may leave.
[Mrs Corrigan stalks out angrily and the bench retires.]

In challenging the magistrate's interpretation of the situation with
her son, Mrs Corrigan presented a problem for control over the translation process. The final power of the magistrate was displayed in his
ability to override Mrs Corrigan's account of her difficulties. The
organizational routine of the court has a built in series of conventions
which enable the authoritative figures – the magistrates and the clerk –
to control the boundaries of the interaction. They are able to make
decisions about what is relevant or not relevant, what is admissible (for
example as a reason for not paying costs as one sum) or not. At the
same time however, because their power rests on organizational *conventions*, it requires compliance, and is therefore always potentially
open to threat. Thus much of the court hearing involves the authority
figures in maintaining control over routines.

The defendant and his/her parent/s are disadvantaged in the court
by their lack of control over such routines but nevertheless always
present a potential, if not an actual, threat of disorder. Ultimately, Mrs
Corrigan had no option but to accept the court's decision, but at the
same time she was able to challenge the logic of the magistrate, the
smooth running of court business, delay the conclusion of the case and
visibly embarrass the chair. Thus juveniles themselves, and to a lesser
extent parents, present a potential source of difficulty for the smooth
running of the translation process, and a good deal of energy is ex-
pended by the other groups of actors to:

1 silence defendants when it seems they might resist enrolment;
2 encourage defendants, where they are engaged in dialogue at all, to
   actively facilitate enrolment by making utterances appropriate to
   the vocabulary of integration and control.

These strategies are necessary for successful translation, for as Law
comments, 'control is quite impossible if translated objects continually
drop out of role' (1986). Compliance is extracted from juveniles as
other actors convince them that it is in their own interests (i.e. in
terms of securing a 'more lenient' sentence) to try and meet magistrates' expectations. Whether it is through drilled bodies ('stand up
straight') or speech acts ('say you're sorry'), this compliance is seen as
important by social workers, solicitors and 'clued up' parents: 'you will
get a better deal if you behave/speak this way'.

Compliance is regarded, in general, as important by all participants.
Magistrates certainly noticed when compliance was absent, as with the

boy who made the mistake of saying that he kicked a bus shelter window through 'for a laugh' ('if that is your attitude to this offence, then you had better get representation'), and the boy who stood apparently defiantly (the magistrate commented 'it was the way he looked at us, as if we were nobody to be dealt with'). Clearly this relates to the emphasis on the attitudes content of social information representations in magistrates' accounts. The attitude (or degree of compliance in the translation process) of the defendant thus has a dual importance. A minimum degree of cooperation is necessary in that it forms a crucial stage in the translation process. The degree of compliance, however, also acts as an important control indicator in magistrates' activities of classifying offenders. Beyond the requirement for compliance, defendants occupy a very minor part in the proceedings; categorization proceeds chiefly on the basis of inscriptions (SIRs, school reports, lists of previous findings of guilt etc.) and verbal interactions between representatives (solicitors, social workers and to a lesser extent parents) and magistrates. The major input by juveniles was in the form of the visual data of comportment. It is this very absence of the 'real' defendant which reveals the project of classification and also reveals the ideological character of juvenile processing. Callon remarked of the relationship between scallops and scientists that:

> The scallops are transformed into larvae, the larvae into numbers, the numbers into tables and curves which represent easily transportable, reproducible, and diffusable sheets of paper . . . the scallops have been displaced . . . a handful of researchers discuss a few diagrams and a few tables with numbers in a closed room. But these discussions commit . . . silent actors . . . three individuals come to speak for the scallops.
>
> Callon 1986: 217–18

Just as a graph or a number is immensely more tractable and durable (Law 1986) than a scallop, so a social inquiry report or a solicitor's standardly phrased speech is more tractable than an incommunicative juvenile or, indeed, a whole population of juveniles. For when one juvenile is processed, in one sense all juveniles are processed. Again, to quote Callon:

> A few larvae are considered to be the official representatives of an anonymous mass of scallops which silently and elusively lurk on the ocean floor. The three [researchers] negotiate the interessement of the scallops through a handful of larvae which represent all the uncountable others that evade captivity.
>
> Callon 1986: 214

So the juvenile in court stands proxy for a whole host of unruly children somewhere 'out there', where discipline has gone out of the window and the family group is disintegrating, those anonymous uncountable scallops roaming the streets. By negotiating the interessement of a few, the agents of 'justice' and 'welfare' achieve control of the many. To return for a moment to Foucault:

> The examination, surrounded by all its documentary techniques, makes each individual a 'case': a case which at one and the same time constitutes an object for a branch of knowledge and a hold for a branch of power . . . the individual as he may be described, judged, measured, compared with others . . . who has to be trained or corrected, classified, normalized, or excluded . . .
>
> Foucault 1977: 191

The existence of the case enables the anonymous mass to be counted, understood and controlled – or more accurately, to be accounted for in that way. It is of little relevance whether the children are actually roaming the streets, whether the short, sharp, shock really deters, whether the supervision order really persuades the child to adopt 'constructive' leisure pursuits as long as the public appearance is one of control, integration and effectiveness. The processes of classification and translation themselves both help to create and sustain a rendering of reality in which the individual case may be diagnosed, a pathology created, a 'solution' proposed, and which in its very individuality indicates a relationship with the overall corpus of unruly youth. This offender is situated in relation to that offender; this one is not a lost cause, that one is a hardened offender . . . Similarly one penalty implies the whole hierarchy of penalties. Through the whole business of processing juveniles, very little attention is paid by participating actors to the *validity* of the social background representations invoked.

No desire is shown to understand the meaning of the offence from the child's point of view; rather the child must account for it in the court's terms (Why did you do it? Did you know it was wrong?). Little interest is shown in whether locking children up in detention centres actually has an effect on behaviour, few questions are asked as to whether or not the whole package of an escalating penalty may not successively reinforce the likelihood of the juvenile's being reintroduced into the 'system' (cf. Cohen 1985).

The emphasis is on describability. The individual is transposed into a set of knowledge representations which are comprehensible not with reference to the actual lived experience and actions of the individual but rather with reference to the instrumentality of those representations: what it is that they enable, and what it is that they preclude. In this sense, Shaun, and Ian, and Nicola, and Michelle themselves, are irrelevant to the juvenile court; 'social information' does not refer to them as people but to the project of the juvenile court in reconstructing them as information objects, entities amenable to processing. Social information simplifies individuals and reduces them to docile figures on sheets of paper (Law 1986: 1).

Thus classification takes away the actual individuality of defendant and the circumstances of his or her life and replaces it with a spurious individuality consisting of a series of attributes capable of judgement; Law's 'docile figures'. The potentially most unruly of the resources is the juvenile her or himself, hence their particular insertion into the business of sentencing. The simultaneous enrolment and silencing of the child is both an expression of, and necessary to, the effective deployment of power.

CHAPTER 7

On easy money? Solicitors and social data

This chapter is concerned with the question of how solicitors generate and deploy social information representations during the sentencing process. Particular emphasis is placed upon examining how the defendant is 'reconstructed' by solicitors. This is seen to be shaped by solicitors' predictions of how magistrates will operate and the conventions of the juvenile court. Related to this is the solicitors' interest in upholding a construction of themselves as 'credible professionals'. It will be argued that the use of social data by solicitors is again part of a process whereby the defendant is continually distanced from the sentencing process and reconstructed as a case amenable to conventional processing. First, however, it is useful to examine magistrates' perceptions of solicitors.

Magistrates' responses to prosecution solicitors tended to be unambiguous, to the extent that they rarely perceived the prosecution as being involved with social data at all. It was generally accepted that prosecutors were simply giving an outline of the facts and that it was defence solicitors who handled social data through their incorporation into the mitigation formula. Only one magistrate commented that 'They are both coloured in what they say by their particular jobs'. Otherwise, the assumption was typically made that the prosecutor was the more objective representative whereas the defence solicitor was more likely to be seen as obviously having an 'axe to grind' and to explicitly present social data to this end.

One of the commonest types of observation made by magistrates was that defence solicitors tend to reiterate the material in the SIR and to represent it as a mitigation plea. Magistrates thus tended to exhibit a degree of scepticism about the value of the solicitor in terms of an input into the sentencing process:

The solicitor's only trying to get them off . . . maybe there's an odd time when I might think, well, yes, because he's said that then . . . I might change my mind . . . but I'd be looking much more in to the social inquiry report.

Sometimes this attitude became incorporated into the routine of the court, so that certain chairpersons would bypass the solicitor altogether if they agreed with the report's recommendation:

If I find that the recommendation is one that I can approve of, and one that I can follow, then I turn to the defence solicitor before he gets to his speech and tell him [and they] tend not to address us at all then, which is sensible.

However, several magistrates, including some who expressed the view that defence solicitors mostly 'go by the SIR', did emphasize that solicitors could *on occasion* bring out information which was not in the SIR, or could correct inaccuracies in the SIR.

They are useful so long as you bear in mind the bias. They do bring information in that is not in the SIR . . . that applied to a case within the last fortnight here.

It depends on how long they've known the family, because quite often, these solicitors have long standing relationships with families . . . and get to know them better and longer [than the social worker] . . . they're a help, yes, because they're family friends, you might say, and certainly as to putting light onto the offences . . . they are helpful.

Thus the defence solicitor could be seen as adding to or updating the data in the SIR; but it seems that for most magistrates, it was their reading of the social inquiry report which would constitute the central plank of their picture-building activities in relation to the offender.

The comments above, however, may be qualified in that magistrates' willingness to accord influence to the 'social information' represented by solicitors depended on their view of the professional competence of particular solicitors and the relationship which the latter had built up with the bench.

You get to know most of the defence solicitors . . . overall I would say the standard is good. You get to know the various styles and you use your knowledge of him to say, oh yes, well he would say that, or else you might look to him to provide you with useful information.

Solicitors vary in their techniques. Some are good, and some are indifferent.

It depends on the solicitor. Some are much better than others, and you sympathise with them.

Clear distinctions were made between solicitors who were seen to be able, professional, reasonably well prepared and conscientious, and those who were seen as 'on easy money' not making a real effort to present the client's case, poorly briefed and 'just trotting out the usual stock phrases'. The response to the latter on the part of magistrates was more likely to be one of switching off, whereas the former were likely to be taken seriously at least some of the time.

The final category invoked by magistrates in discussing defence solicitors related to the latter's role in facilitating the quick and 'efficient' expedition of cases:

They just use the report and address us . . . but it is useful to have defence solicitors because it saves a lot of time to deal with the solicitors rather than the children and the parents themselves.

The defence solicitor is vital with youngsters because there is so much need for information from the bench and he can do so much sorting out with the parents . . .

It is desirable to have a defence solicitor, because the child and his parents are very often inarticulate.

In a curious way these kinds of comments are extremely relevant to a discussion of the defence solicitor's role in presenting social data to the bench. However much it is standardly phrased, or borrows from the SIR, the defence solicitor's account is seen by these magistrates as better than relying on the parent and the defendant themselves *because it facilitates the smoother running of the court*. The defendant and/or parent would either be inarticulate or may seek to impose an inappropriate message on the court threatening the coherence of the proceedings (see Chapter 6). Hence the concept of a smooth running court is one which avoids the messy raw data, the *actual* defendant, and works instead on the basis of a representation which is in accordance with the conventions of interpretation used by the bench and the conventions of processing adopted in the court. Anomalies in pleas, 'inappropriate' information, can be sifted by the defence solicitor to provide a case which is comprehensible in the court's terms. The solicitor is thus responsible for the prevention of impurities clogging up the classification and disposition of offenders and delaying or threatening effective translation (cf. Chapter 1).

How were solicitors observed to operate in practice? Before discussing the observation data it is worth noting that the findings of the present study in this respect largely corroborate those of Parker *et al.* (1981) and Williamson (1980). Williamson found that in presenting mitigation pleas the solicitor becomes an expert witness, adding social arguments to more narrowly legal arguments (Williamson 1980: 39). He noted the use of typical social background ingredients in mitigation addresses, such as 'good home background (especially effective parental control)', 'bad company', 'recognition of severity of offence and remorse', 'adverse effect of dispositions', and 'turning point, critical stage in life' (*ibid* 46–8).

Parker *et al.* (1981) also recognized the use of these stories but added that their deployment was more complex in that solicitors usually operated such background factors strategically, within their assessment of the tariff score and their knowledge of the operational rules of their particular bench (1981: 59). Indeed, in Parker's study, 'City's' solicitors were seen as being so closely in tune with the bench's sentencing policy that they could be seen as part of an "integral feedback loop" ' (*ibid*) which reinforced bench practices. Both Parker and Williamson found that solicitors were always aware of their need to retain credibility with the bench; and Williamson further argues that it is the process of representation which relegates the defendant to the part of the 'dummy player' (cf. Carlen 1976) to the point where

> Many mitigating arguments bear little resemblance to the offender's true circumstances and appear to be no more than a technical construction of points which the solicitor believes will be effective before certain magistrates.
>
> Williamson 1980: 48

The discussion of the observation data in this chapter supports these comments; to some extent it will go further by suggesting that the very distancing of which Williamson writes is integral to the operation of juvenile justice in a more fundamental way than its use in the immediate tactics of mitigation. It is closely bound in with the overall pattern of the social relations of juvenile justice, with the enterprise of classification as a technique of power.

It is important that the prosecuting solicitor is the first to state his or her version of the offence and the offender. Social information representations are generated implicitly as the prosecutor typically engages in the business of steering the magistrates towards the appropriate outcome. The prosecutor's choice of language can make a substantial difference to the 'version' of the offender and it was usually clear when the prosecutor was pushing towards the 'heavy end', regarding the offender as hard core. The prosecution account is thus important in setting the tone for the subsequent processing of the defendant. In general a slightly bored, sparse, account using very few scene-setting devices and giving very little context beyond the location of the offence and the details of the apprehension, the value of stolen property, and other matters heralded an obvious, soft end case. Here exchanges would be brief and the whole hearing would be characterized by nods and implicit agreement, with very little actually said and little conflict.

In contrast, heavy end cases, where the prosecution was clearly attempting to push the defendant 'over the edge' would involve a long and complex prosecution account of five minutes or more. Extensive details would be given concerning the context of the offence, about the defendant's reaction to their apprehension, and the previous record of offending and TICs. Rather than simply referring to an event 'happening', picturesque adjectives would be invoked, tending to produce images of the breakdown of law and order, threat to the community (particularly the 'weak and defenceless') and the intransigent wickedness of the offender.

Thus in a case where a boy was charged with theft of a chocolate bar and seven TICs the prosecution account was kept fairly sparse and low key, simply stating that the defendant was 'apprehended taking a bar of chocolate from the supermarket by a floor manager' and that on tape the boy had admitted to taking it. The boy was not represented and it seemed taken for granted by everyone that the outcome was an 'obvious' CD. The case was processed in less than five minutes, magistrates skimmed the reports, did not bother retiring and nodded to each other. They briefly asked the boy, then his parents, if they had anything to say, did not pursue their monosyllabic replies but moved quickly to disposal.

This contrasted sharply with the prosecutor's treatment of heavy end cases, where contextual information was articulated in such a way as to present a clear incorrigible. The following account relates to a girl pleading guilty to a burglary charge:

> The defendant entered the house by the window. The premises were completely ransacked and £740 worth of property taken. The defendant has a number of further matters, all involving preying on defenceless elderly people . . . she seems to make a habit of taking property as and when she pleases. The officers who interviewed her said that she seemed amused. In this particular case, Mr [ ] had left home for some hours . . . his wife has

senile dementia and this is known to the children in the area.
The defendant was seen entering the house with two others.
The juveniles had also entered another property, and they have
admitted a number of other offences, victimising elderly and
infirm people . . .

Here the prosecutor stressed the forced entry, the habitual offending behaviour, the concept of deliberately 'preying upon' the elderly,
the group nature of the offences, the unrepentant attitude of the
defendant, the calculated nature of the offence, the value of the property and the destruction caused.

Another such attempt at pushing the defendant 'down the slippery
slope' was less successful, partly because the defence solicitor had a
particularly strong counter-account. The boy in question was charged
with causing bodily harm by 'wantonly and furiously driving' a motorcycle upon common land. It was clear from the pre-court discussion
that the prosecution considered this a 'good bet' for a custodial sentence
and wanted to get the case off the books, as it had been adjourned
several times already. When the case got under way, the prosecutor
confidently mobilized his account, emphasizing the speed at which the
defendant was driving the motorcycle across common land:

> He then deliberately aimed the motorcycle at a group of youn-
> ger children walking along the path and drove amongst them.
> He hit a four year old child who sustained a very nasty bump to
> the head and was taken to hospital. It was fortunate that the
> child was not more seriously injured.

What the prosecuting solicitor had not counted upon, however,
was the ability of the defence solicitor to erect a strongly counter-
manding version of events:

> Guy had obtained the motorcycle only the day before the inci-
> dent. He was riding around for most of the day. Guy's version is
> not a great deal different from my friend's – except that he was
> riding for a gap between the groups of people and not riding at
> anyone – it is what you might call a technical offence. The
> report (SIR) itself is balanced and reasonable: the lad has ob-
> viously been in trouble in the past, but I ask you to view it like
> this. He was sorry for what happened, he did not intend it to
> happen, he actually went back and helped the boy and saw that
> he was attended to. That is not the attitude of somebody who
> didn't care. He leaves school at Easter and takes his CSEs, and
> . . . I would ask you to let the supervision order continue and
> impose a financial penalty.

The report, meanwhile, had suggested that the boy had committed previous offences while living with his mother; he was now living a 'more settled family life' under the control of his father and stepmother.

The prosecution attempt to force Guy down the slippery slope clearly failed for the magistrates imposed a £40 fine and allowed the supervision order to continue. While the prosecution had invoked intentionality, disregard for others, viciousness and the vulnerability of the victim, the defence solicitor was able to counteract this with a denial of intentionality, concern for the victim and 'improvements' in behaviour and attitudes drawing on SIR data, as well as a more 'structured and controlled' home life. Thus the prosecution accounts begin the process of attempting to reconstitute the defendant in to a particular type of defendant; their accounts were in no sense purely factual but aimed at presented a social being for consideration by the justices.

Thus in the adversarial process defendants themselves and the complex situational events surrounding the offence(s) begin to be scaled down, scaled up and redrawn in schematic form in a way that enabled 'justice to be done' – seriousness could be assessed, weighed against intentionality, balanced with the damage to the victim, tempered by the attitude of the offender . . . It is then the business of the defence solicitor to reverse the impetus which the prosecutor has set in motion by using the same data in different ways, or by selecting different data for scaling up, so as to present a different picture of the defendant.

Defence solicitors were chiefly found to operate on their working knowledge of the routine practice of the court and of the tariff and on their 'knowledge' of the hardness or softness of certain justices (i.e. justice's preferences for certain disposals and the point at which they would be likely to invoke the 'punitive philosophy'). They quickly identified control indicators in social data which they felt justices would respond to. In doing this they attempted to destructure the prosecution account and to restructure it. Nor is it quite accurate to suggest that solicitors simply 'crib' the SIR – rather they use it selectively and reframe the selected portions, sometimes producing a quite different sort of picture from the same basic data by decontextualizing it. The more energetic defence solicitors, or those who had an association going back some time with the family, would seek other background data directly from their clients which would help them in this task.

The positive control indicators mobilized by defence solicitors did in fact broadly match those indicators defined as central by magistrates, so in this sense defence solicitors were reading the agenda accurately, i.e. they concentrated on signs of family 'stability and control', 'constructive' leisure interests, prospects of employment, interest in joining the armed forces, attitude to the offence, lack of culpability due to the influence of undesirable older friends/acquaintances. These would be related in specific ways to the tariff status of the case in hand.

Defence accounts are now examined in relation to these control indicators as mitigating factors in more detail.

Home and family background

Common usages within this category were, first, an attempt to promote an image of control within the home background:

> Sensible measures have been taken within the household. [ ] is now living under a very strict regime . . .

> A friend of the family in his late twenties now lives upstairs and is taking [ ] under his wing. He is involving him in healthy outdoor activities and has recently been taking him walking and so on out in the Lake District

Alternatively, however, where the defence solicitor was attempting a holding operation on the tariff by arguing for supervision in the community, a lack of control might be stressed, but in conjunction with the family's willingness to accept agency intervention:

> There is no male member of the family. He is wandering around getting into mischief, he is an immature boy and needs somebody else to assist him.

> The home background does show a lack of direction. Mrs [ ] and [ ] agree to cooperate fully with social services.

> The parents are anxious to get whatever help they can with the boys. The background is excellent, indeed it is difficult to understand why they are deviant. I would say that the attitude of the parents is most hopeful.

Williamson's 'crucial stage of life' category might also be invoked here:

> We need to be concerned about the transition of this young man into adulthood. He has had a tragic experience with his mother and an unhappy experience of abuse with his father. The social workers are working very hard and making headway . . . we need to consider very carefully whether we should interrupt his transition from care into learning to look after himself in his own bedsit.

In this case, the image was clearly implied that it was the direct influence of the family which 'caused' offending, but that the defendant was taking positive steps to become a 'decent citizen' outside of that environment. This was another case in which the prosecution lost what they felt was a 'clear custodial'.

In a more general sense solicitors might stress the 'excellent family background' or 'caring supportive parents' – usually, it seemed, when they had been unwilling to expend a great deal of trouble on the case, because it was relatively soft end or because they could find no specific data to support particular control indicators.

Leisure and hobbies

[ ] has reached an excellent standard in football and rugby. He has played in his school and local teams. There is a great deal to build on in this young man.

He's a healthy young man with healthy interests . . . [goes on to describe defendant's interest in falconry].

[ ] is very interested in Art . . . he has recently helped with the murals for the [local music festival] – your worships may have noticed his photograph in the local paper.

The above examples are illustrative of the (fairly rare) cases where solicitors were able to use social data to evoke a measure of constructive, socially integrative, use of leisure time. On a number of occasions a boy's interest in joining the armed forces was put forward. These accounts were clearly used to show the defendants' potential given a non-custodial disposal, their attachment and commitment to normal values, their ability to contribute to, rather than threaten, social order. This contrasts to the statement made by one defence solicitor regarding his client:

He doesn't do much in his spare time. He is one of the aimless young men patrolling the area.

Consistent with the implications of the above utterance, the defendant received a rather long custodial sentence. The solicitor had not wished to risk his credibility by attempting to promote a positive view of his client in what everyone appeared to regard as a hopeless case.

School/work

Defence solicitors regarded any positive control indicators relating to school and work to be particularly 'strong' (i.e. influential) points. Especially in a context where the vast majority of defendants were either unemployed or were 'cooled out' of school, then a positive school report or definite career aim, offer of work, or a good YTS scheme, were used by solicitors. They could be presented as evidence of potential for 'reform' into acceptance of the normative social structure and of commitment to the integrative values of work discipline, 'getting on', 'steadiness' and 'prospects' (i.e. of becoming a 'decent', stable, adult):

> John is a very intelligent boy. He has had problems at school but his attitude has now improved, and he sat his 'O' levels without any further problems. He wishes to pursue an FE course in September . . .

> There is a lot of good in Dayle. Indeed, when his YTS came to an end, his employer persuaded the YTS to let Dayle remain with him.

> Both boys are working . . . and the employer has provided a very good reference for Alan which is presented to the court.

Again, the occasional situation arose when the solicitor appeared to state his lack of intention to prevent his client's slide down 'the slope':

> Like so many boys nowadays, Jason is unemployed and seems to lack any structure or aim.

Attitudes

Defence solicitors were well aware that magistrates sought to manufacture attitude representations from social data and very few solicitors failed to evoke some image of penitence or willingness to submit to authority by their clients.

> Kevin is basically not a bad lad at all. He is polite, and responds well to discipline.

> Carl is very sorry and has spent the intervening three weeks very worried. Apart from the educational hiccup he is a responsible young man. He has caused great inconvenience to everyone and apologises profusely.

This corresponds to control indicators and mitigating factors sought by magistrates, and once more reflects the knowledge of solicitors of their court.

Circumstances/seriousness of the offence

Somewhat in contrast to social inquiry reports defence solicitors stressed the specific circumstances leading up to a commission of an offence. This could be, at times, a very important plank in the defence solicitor's attempt to counter the prosecution evocation of incorrigibility, intentionality and culpability. Defence accounts typically attempted to reconstrue the offence as less serious and as less criminal by deprecating the effects of the offence on the victim or its value in money or the incorrigibility of the offender. Sometimes the technical or quasi-accidental nature of the offence would be stressed.

> It is incorrect to talk of him as a 'lookout' as it wasn't premeditated.

> He took his mother's money because his friend threatened him. He is now deeply sorry.

> The present offence cannot be condoned. But there are two categories, in general, of criminal damage; where it causes destruction, or causes spoiling. The TIC in this case involved writing his name in felt tip pen on a window frame.

> These were very much spur of the moment offences.

> I would like to place this matter in context . . . remarks were made about the adult's father by the complainant and Higgins became involved and was arrested at the scene largely because of his abusive language . . . (boy charged with S5 Breach of the Peace)

Thus in the sense that prosecution accounts would typically seek to portray the premeditated and serious nature of the offences, and defence solicitors would seek to mobilize additional data which would place a 'context' around the circumstances of the offence which deflected its seriousness, solicitors occupied classical adversarial roles. The only marked exceptions to this were in court B, where cases were observed in which prosecution and defence accounts complemented each other; and in all courts where a cut and dried custody case was involved.

Recommendations

In most cases defence solicitors would be urging the justices to follow social inquiry report recommendations. In a minority of cases they would seek to secure a disposal somewhat down tariff of the SIR. In both cases they placed their arguments not only within legal constraints or arguments of just retribution but within the context of the assumed tariff structure. Defence accounts would also seek to inject a note of hopefulness as to the 'effect' of the suggested disposal on the defendant and also often add financial information to support their case.

> A supervision order with IT has been recommended. I have talked to the social worker and we hope that that would give him the necessary discipline. Steven fully appreciates the gravity of his situation and that you may be considering DC or YC.

> I suggest that you give him the chance urged in the recommendations – a deferred sentence for 3 months with IT during this period. As I said to him outside this court, if he doesn't stop now, he's locking himself up.

> In this case of Jones, it is obviously of concern that he's growing cannabis and is arrested drunk late at night. But he has seen what happens to criminals, and I would urge you to follow the recommendation. He needs that discipline and the satisfaction of having done something useful.

> Your worships have four sentencing options: a CD; a financial penalty, – but that would fall on the parents; an AC order, he's had that before, or, and this may be in the forefront of your minds, a custodial sentence. But you must take into account the criteria laid down in the 1982 Criminal Justice Act. Firstly, the protection of the public; well, he did abscond from care but he didn't offend. Second, non-response to other measures; [care institution] say in the report that he has made excellent progress. Or that the offence is so serious that no other option is feasible; well, all offences are serious, but these are not of the most serious.

Solicitors assess the available data for its potential and represent it to the magistrates in a way which they judge will coincide with the justices' search for control indicators. Part of this process is that the solicitors attempt to empathize with the magisterial perspective – 'of course this is serious'; 'I understand that you may be thinking of custody'; 'there can be no excuse'; 'they knew what they were doing' – followed by the inevitable 'but'.

A sizeable minority of defence solicitors observed in the study, however, clearly spent little time with their clients. They would quickly skim through the reports and simply state in mitigation that they would 'urge your worships to follow the recommendations' and sit down again. Similarly, as frequently occurred in courts A and E, when a chairman simply announced that 'we are minded to follow the recommendations' before the defence solicitor had addressed the bench, she or he would typically acknowledge this and sit down again.

Second, defence solicitors, especially in court E, would be mindful of their reputation with the bench and of their overall caseload. Defence solicitors did not relish being in a position where 'muggins has got to stand up and ask for more CSO' (defence solicitor's comment on a 'hopeless case'). Where the SIR contained no clear recommendation and clearly implied custody (or in a small number of cases actually recommended custody) – where the defendant was clearly set to be 'pushed off the end of the slippery slope' – defence solicitors would either explicitly, or through implicit signifiers such as tone of voice, 'code words' and brevity of address, concur in this outcome.

Defence solicitors clearly worked within the limits of what they perceived to be the implicit working rules of their own courts, seeing their jobs best fulfilled in knowing what they could and could not 'get away with' with prosecutors and magistrates. This was recognized by all sides. As one magistrate commented:

> [Defence solicitor] is an experienced man and he knew he wouldn't get away with a supervision order, so when he started his address I shook my head just ever so slightly and he immediately changed his tack and started arguing for an attendance centre order . . .

Similarly where a recommendation for an attendance centre order had been made, a defence solicitor felt that he would 'not get away with it'. The offence was assault involving a broken nose, and in mitigation the solicitor argued against the SIR, asking for CSO, thus moving his client several runs 'up the ladder' from an SIR recommendation which was perceived by all to be totally unrealistic and likely to result in custody.

The business of the court is dominated by what is usual, and while that may be negotiated the limits of the tariff are continually reproduced by and at the same time embodied in the organizational practices of the court. Social data as articulated by solicitors enable the business of classifying offenders into tariff categories to go ahead: for solicitors, social workers and magistrates need to be able to produce a soft end and a hard end in order to accomplish their routine activities within the boundaries of what is normal. In the sense that magistrates rely heavily on other sources of social data (see the early part of this chapter) to manufacture social information, the defence solicitors' presentation of data is perhaps of little importance. Interviews with magistrates suggested that unless the solicitor came up with something 'fresh', then his/her contribution was mainly window dressing. But behind the window dressing lies another function, perhaps more important than the effect of mitigation on decisions. That is the role of the solicitor as one of Callon's intermediaries (1986). The defence solicitor is someone who speaks 'for' the defendant. Through the use of the 'representative', the defendant is silenced, reality is distanced and the 'real' business of the court can go smoothly ahead, for 'to speak for others is first to silence those in whose name we speak (Callon 1986: 216; see also Chapter 1).

Perhaps the solicitor, rather than representing the defendant in the true sense, is also part of the process of the 'mobilisation of allies' (Callon 1986), an alignment of the social relations of the juvenile justice system which by its very nature excludes the realities of everyday experiences in the world outside. Chapter 6 discussed the threat which defendants could pose to the translation process and through that to the microsystem of power in the courtroom. This threat is neutralized as defence solicitors become locked into a holy alliance with magistrates.

CHAPTER 8

Sentencing and social structure

We must form an opinion as to whether he's a real idiot, going slowly over the edge and becoming a real villain, then we would suggest something fairly severe . . .

The relationship between social information and the sentencing process is chiefly characterized by magistrates' concern with the control of unruly youth. If the juvenile court is riven by a contradiction between the principles of welfare and justice this was not apparent in the sentencing practices of magistrates (Clarke 1985). Even where magistrates used the concepts of welfare and justice, they could not be conflated with the use of such terminology in the discourses of social work or penal philosophy. 'Welfare' disposals such as supervision orders were sometimes justified as having a punishment content, and 'punitive' disposals such as detention centre orders were sometimes justified as having a 'welfare' component. 'Welfare' was typically interpreted as 'the best interests of the child', which in no way ruled out punitive disposals as far as magistrates were concerned ('spare the rod and spoil the child', as one justice commented).

Hence the use of social information did not import welfare considerations into sentencing. Rather, the welfare content of reports was translated into control indicators and thus rendered congruent with the disciplinary conventions of the juvenile court.

Social information and the socialized tariff

The transformation of social data into control indicators can only be fully understood in the context of the operation of what may be termed a *socialized tariff* in the juvenile court. This form of tariff sentencing does not play off justice factors against welfare factors; such an interpretation misconceives the nature of sentencing in the juvenile court. The tariff in the juvenile court is not simply a progression of disposals in proportion to acts, which may then be tempered by welfare need. It is a progression in relation to *delinquencies*.

Magistrates are basically concerned with locating offenders on a slippery slope or ladder of dispositions culminating in custody: 'they work their way up the ladder until the inevitable happens', or 'they're on the brink of the slippery slope'. As we have seen, magistrates identify their task as one of deciding whereabouts on the slope the offender is currently positioned: is it youthful high spirits; has she or he become a hardened offender; is she or he destined for a life of crime? However, the positioning of the offender on the slippery slope will always be intimately connected with social imagery; for 'it is not just his act, but his life' which is relevant in characterizing him or her (Foucault 1977: 251). For the juvenile court magistrate it is not just the offender's act which is at issue but his or her life. Magistrates sought to identify those who might still, with 'help', be able to become good citizens. It is this which informed magistrates' search for control indicators and which explains the dominance of concerns with notions of discipline, physical ability, industriousness, a kind of moral and physical hygiene (Joseph and Fritsch 1977). The good citizen plays

> the game honestly for the good of the whole . . . you discipline and put yourself readily and willingly at the service of constituted authority for the main good. The best disciplined community is the happiest community . . . there must be many . . . a fine young fellow dragged down by bad influences around him . . . he can rise above his surroundings and paddle his way to success.
>
> Baden-Powell 1930: 220,227

The tariff in the juvenile court is socialized because every act implies a kind of person and every social background image implies something about the nature of the act. Thus it is not possible to separate components such as 'seriousness of offence' and weigh it against 'social background'.

As Emerson comments, 'Typical delinquencies also identify the kind of typical actor because they include a picture of the kind of youth who is apt to be involved in this kind of performance' (Emerson 1969: 108). The term 'socialized tariff' is thus a formalized version of the slippery slope. It is not a question only of proportionality to the offence in the juvenile court but of proportionality to the delinquency. At the extremes of transgression social imagery is read off from the offence data: the 'kind of youth' is taken for granted from the 'kind of offence'. Only a 'real villain' who is 'beyond the bounds of control' would burgle and despoil an old person's bungalow. Such a person is *de facto* beyond help. In less extreme cases, however, additional social indicators are sought from other sources: from reports, from the juveniles and parents themselves, from solicitors. The most complex decision processes occurred over decisions between fine or supervision, supervision or attendance centre; intensive intermediate treatment or custody: these were the grey area cases where magistrates would try to identify the degree of hope from an offender's social background data. Social control indicators are the cues which justices extract from social data in order to help position defendants on the slippery slope; the whole range of data from the reported circumstances of the offence, through the juvenile's demeanour in court, to the social inquiry report, act as a resource which can:

1 Seal the fate of an offender whose record already suggests she or he is incorrigible, headed for the end of the slippery slope:

> When you looked at the gravity of the offences, and the boys attitude, he didn't co-operate with the police or his mother, he committed offences whilst on bail . . . (3 months' DC)

2 Suggest salvable elements in the defendant's life or personality which offer a potential for 'pulling them back from the edge':

> It was a serious offence [burglary] and he is getting help with the solvent abuse and the parents were obviously sensible . . . he had a job and it seemed worth a try . . . (Fine)

3 Suggest dangerous elements in the defendant's life or personality which *despite* the apparent soft endedness implied by the offence, suggest that she or he is 'really' headed for trouble: 'If that is your attitude to this offence [criminal damage – bus shelter] you had better get yourself representation. (adjourned – considering custody)

The slippery slope is not just concerned with punishing legal transgressions but transgressions of social discipline of which criminal offences are only one symptom among many. Moreover, the socialized tariff is essentially bifurcatory. All courts, though they varied in the length of the slope and the degree of its slipperiness, operated a continuum of distinctions, gradations of salvability, with a final break between the hard core and those whom 'something might be done with'. It is not that 'deeds' were weighed against 'needs' to produce some sort of compromise; nor that in some cases disciplinary issues were weighed against offence issues. All decisions were informed by disciplinary considerations and all decisions involved a consideration of social information, whether that came from reports or by implication from the perceived nature of the offence.

To describe the operation of the socialized tariff is a relatively easy matter. The more complex task is to explain why it is produced and reproduced through the routine practices of sentencing. Magistrates experience the socialized tariff as a reality, as a structure within which they have no other choice but to work. Yet at the same time, as powerful agents, they clearly choose to operate according to the principle of the socialized tariff. The remainder of this chapter will thus seek to deconstruct the given nature of the tariff, and to redefine it as *accomplished*, for as Giddens comments, 'All structural properties of social systems . . . are the medium and outcome of the contingently accomplished activities of situated actors . . . (Giddens 1984: 191).

Three closely related themes are particularly important in understanding the production of the socialized tariff in the juvenile court.

Routinization and institutionalization

The interaction of the courtroom itself, as has been well documented (Cicourel 1976; Parker *et al.* 1981; Carlen 1976) occurs largely in patterned and routinized ways based on implicit rules and background expectancies within which practices are situated. Action occurs typically at the level of taken for granted assumptions. Thus magistrates might try to push the decision a point or two one way or the other but on the whole they implicitly accepted the tariff as a mode of producing juvenile justice. In this sense the weight of history continually lies behind the production of the tariff. It is not simply determined by the magistrates themselves but is actively re-created every time the court sits. The routine activities of processing juveniles, involving interlocking expectations of solicitors, social workers, magistrates and juveniles and parents themselves, are played out on the basis of yesterday's stories.

Thus many magistrates described the sensation of becoming case hardened which grew with experience of sitting on the bench, along with an ability to 'read between the lines'. They formed expectations of social workers, court officers, solicitors and each other, which governed the way in which they perceived a case; formed 'schools of opinion' about the utility of particular local resources, about local problems; and implicitly or explicitly, suggested the existence of a bench 'ethos':

There are many ways of dealing with an offence, we might have the same view of an offence but a different view of its resolution

> . . . I have seen YC and think its valuable, whereas [colleague] is strongly pro-DC.

> If it had just been [colleague] I could have moved her, she's fairly new and I could have leaned on her, but [ ] is a hard man and he's been on the bench a long time, I couldn't lean on him heavily enough.

> You always sit together. Now there's a great danger in that, because then . . . you could find yourself getting a pattern of sentencing coming out . . . there's just a danger that you'll get more of a sympathico with people that you're used to.

The concept of a bench ethos may be seen not only as referring to patterns of sentencing or preferences for particular dispositions, but to the kind of folk wisdom shared in retiring rooms, over coffee and on social occasions. Such folk wisdom may concern local 'notorious families', views about the origins of offending, local 'problems', views of agencies and so on.

The strongest benchlore concerned the hard core. Magistrates reinforced each others' beliefs in the hard core of offenders whom nothing but custody could touch; the 'regular villains'; 'our regulars'; 'the ones who come back time and again'. They typically held shared (and therefore mutually constructed) views about the phenomenon of the hard end (or hardened) offender who 'repeatedly burgled old peoples' bungalows'; about first offenders 'not being first offenders these days; they are already criminals when they come to us':

> We have our regulars . . . well, we have our faces we see time and again. Then they go on and you see them in the adult court . . .

> They come to us as first offenders . . . only they aren't really because they've usually had three or four cautions . . .

Thus magistrates, while experiencing the tariff as structure, actively create that structure both in the routine exchanges of doing justice and in the informal cultural milieu which exists around the edges of the formal court setting. While their power is always temporary in that it relies on the compliance of other agents, magistrates are the strongest force in the translation process. This does not mean that they are impervious to influence through the daily negotiation of justice either from each other or from other members of the holy alliances formed in juvenile processing (i.e. with social workers, probation officers, the police). But the very routinization of juvenile processing involves the power of magistrates as controlling agents:

A routine may be thought of as a potential or capacity, to be set in operation or not, pointed this way or that, . . . at the discretion of the controlling agent. Such an agent possesses social power. The possession of power is the possession of discretion . . .

Barnes 1988: 58

Thus as Giddens argues:

Power relations are often most profoundly embedded in modes of conduct which are taken for granted by those who follow them, most especially in routinized behaviour, which is only diffusely motivated.

Giddens 1984: 176

In order to properly understand the way in which magistrates appear to act in order to constrain themselves by creating the tariff, it is necessary to understand that the structural rules of the tariff are the basis of magistrates' power.

While constraining magistrates the tariff mode of sentencing also allows them discretion; the power to categorize; to invoke social information representations; to articulate conceptions of the way the world is and to impose them on others. Thus the following justices' clerk, while acknowledging his influence in shaping the tariff, also recognized the limits of that influence:

When you advise the magistrates on what is allowable and what is useful you obviously try – I'm not saying it's conscious, but you must have an idea of what the appropriate penalty would be – I'm sure you must try and influence the outcome. There are times when you think they've got to give a custodial sentence for this, if they didn't it would be . . . unusual. I can't say, 'such and such would be an appropriate sentence' . . . but relationships are crucial, your relationship with the chairman . . . it's really very much like being a butler. I really think that's an accurate analogy. Because the butler ran the house, had a lot of power, but in the end had no power, because the man upstairs had the final power, the final say.

Discretion and power

Attention has already focused on the flexibility of such concepts as welfare and punishment as used by magistrates. It is precisely the discretion afforded magistrates within the structural constraints of the tariff which constitutes their power. This is the power to make authoritative definitions which is illustrated by Whitehead and Macmillan in their study of juveniles sentenced to custody under the 1982 Criminal Justice Act criteria of 'seriousness'. 'Seriousness of the offence' was cited as a reason for custody in cases ranging from theft of sweets valued at 36p to four dwelling-house burglaries involving over £1000 and 13 TICs:

> It is clear from these and other examples that the concept of seriousness is used to cover a wide range of offences . . . the word 'seriousness' . . . sometimes seems to be a blank cheque to send juveniles into custody.
>
> Whitehead and Macmillan 1985: 87

As McBarnet has suggested, the very 'layness' and lack of law in the lower courts encourages an erosion of precision in the application of the rules of due process. (McBarnet 1981). The socializing of the tariff in the juvenile court produces even more discretion for it legitimates the deployment of concepts which by their nature are forced to be imprecise. These are the concepts of social information, which relate to a putative normality, a scale of goodness or badness in the family home, for

> What is a 'home situation'? With what degree of assurance may we utter the designations adequate, inadequate, or poor? . . . and what forms of evidence are used to associate or dissociate persons from each of these categories?
>
> Matza 1964: 117

Precisely because the criteria of relevant social information are all inclusive and diffuse (Matza 1964), relating as they do to interpretations of normality, the combination of control indicators based on social data with progressive sentencing severity gives 'rampant discretion' to magistrates. Preceding chapters have described the interpretive conventions which govern the use of social information by magistrates. The relevance of information in the end depends on these kind of interpretive judgements about the 'delinquent' and her or his family:

> What disposition? If we ask court agents, they will honestly and appropriately answer that it depends. On what does it depend? It depends on other factors. On what other factors? Well, perhaps on a diagnosis of the child's personality, but that too depends. On what does that depend? Ultimately, it depends on the needs of the child. And on what do these needs depend? . . . It

> depends on the professional training, experience and judgement of the court agents . . .
>
> Matza 1964: 116

Magistrates control a diffuse and potentially all inclusive discourse through the operation of the socialized tariff. They exercise a real power which is based on their ability to invoke social information categories in support of decisions which in the end rest upon their powers of judgement:

> It's just a question of judgement, really, you learn by experience.
>
> I think a lot of lady magistrates . . . you do things by your intuition.
>
> We're not social workers. We have to use our common sense.
>
> It all comes down to . . . judgement really in the end.

The control over imprecise concepts which the use of social information involves ensures that any challenge to that judgement is particularly difficult. The structure of the bifurcatory tariff is a distinct advantage in the successful exercise of discretionary power, because it creates a facticity of categories – a continuum of salvability to incorrigibility – which justifies the use of social data. In providing the heuristic mechanism by which magistrates allocate offenders on that always already existing bifurcatory slope, control indicators are techniques of power.

(Ir)rationality and the problem of decision making in the juvenile court

Ultimately, however, the techniques of power of the socialized tariff are enabled by the fundamental irrationality which characterizes the most liberal of juvenile courts. The vagueness of the decision concepts with which justices have to work (good/bad home backgrounds etc.) are symptomatic of the lack of substantive rationality in the decision environment within which they work. Strictly speaking, substantive rationality ends the moment when it ceases to be possible to make a computation of the type 'if x, then y' (March and Simon 1970). Even allowing that this is an ideal type rather than something which can be fully realized in most decision situations, it is clear that the magisterial task could never remotely approximate rationality. Rationality demands that goals can be clearly defined, that the means to achieve desired goals can be spelt out and that the means to achieve the desired goals are available to the decision maker.

Magistrates are faced with a highly complex decision environment since ostensibly their goal is to alter the behaviour of human beings. The goal of 'trying to prevent reoffending', 'to protect the public' or 'to help pull him back from the edge' are so diffuse as to create a good deal of uncertainty. This is without even beginning to think about the complexities of not just stopping offending behaviour but reforming a person. Such goals defy clear definition, (What is a 'useful citizen'? What is 'normal'?) let alone the formulation of sensible means to achieve them. There is no possibility of magistrates achieving the kind of global behavioural control which is connoted by such aspirations; there is certainly no 'cure' for juvenile offending which can be achieved through magisterial powers (Cohen 1985).

For magistrates the result of this is to create a decision situation of unbearable uncertainty; the anxiety induced by this kind of phenomenon has been well researched (see Macrimmon 1976 for a review). They are faced with the problem of how to reduce the mass of untidy data 'out there' into something which can be manipulated to resemble decision making of the substantively rational kind demanded by the bureaucratic setting of the court (Matza characterizes the juvenile court as exercising Kadi justice in a bureaucratic setting: Matza 1964: 120). Magistrates are faced with the problem of finding a means by which 'Individual concerns are *transformed* into "workable doctrines" that may routinely function as enlightening guides to action rather than mystifying obstacles' (*ibid*: 125).

Much of this study has been concerned with charting those 'workable doctrines': the interpretive conventions developed by magistrates in the reading of social data, the control indicators derived from the activity of reading, the creation of a socialized tariff. Tariff sentencing lends a rationale to the business of the juvenile court. The institutionalized response to irrationality thus involves magistrates in a number of strategies trying to apply their discretionary power. The tariff creates order from chaos; it lends a sense of form and purpose to what must otherwise be a formless and purposeless activity. The 'goals' are reduced to the achievable ends of allocating offenders along the slippery slope. A series of conventions and rules of thumb are developed to enable offenders to be placed according to their approximations to and deviations from an idealized 'norm'. This enables social data to be utilized effectively as a resource in a way which would otherwise be impossible, for how could the juvenile court, with its small range of punishments, possibly address the 'needs' of the child or the community?

This mode of operating justice has, moreover, the advantage of fitting into the bureaucratic requirement of the court: the case.

Because it is based on a version of the norm it can reduce the mass of uncooperative data about the offender and her/his family into comparable knowledge representations and organize them into the case, an entity which is classifiable within the interpretive conventions of magistrates and which is at the same time indispensable for the courts' internal operation and external legitimation. The case enables justice to be done and enables justice to be seen to be done. In respect of the former, the case quite simply enables messy individuals to be reduced to manipulable elements amenable to bureaucratic processing (Parker *et al.* 1981; Carlen 1976). In respect of the latter, the case has an invaluable ideological function in lending a gloss of equity to court proceedings: the case is impersonal; all cases will receive equality of consideration; the facts of the case will be fully examined.

The process of discretion making in relation to the tariff is rather like placing a tick in a box in a multiple choice question to which there is no right answer. Discretions need only to be judged internally, with reference to the job that they do: ticking the boxes. They do not need to be justified externally, to be able to claim that they have found the right answers (reducing the crime rate, reforming offenders), as long as the minimal requirements of legality (McBarnet 1981) have been met. Discretion making in the juvenile court is possible precisely because it is peculiarly self-sustaining and private; it is not accountable, either to the communities it serves or in terms of its social achievements. If its performance is criticized it can close around itself and refuse to comment; can claim that 'every case is different' or that the critic did not hear all 'the facts'. It is self-validating. This is the power of the magistrate.

The tariff, then, is an institutionalized response to the 'problem' posed by sentencing juveniles. This does not explain why the bifurcatory solution should be the one to be adopted. This is the point at which the structural properties of the juvenile court stretch beyond the immediate boundaries of the courtroom; the tariff is one moment on the 'carceral continuum' (Foucault 1977: 303) which

> Linked, through innumerable relations, the two long, multiple series of the punitive and the abnormal . . . the carceral, with its far reaching networks, allows the recruitment of major 'delinquents'. It organizes what might be called 'disciplinary careers' in which, through various exclusions and rejections, a whole process is set in motion

and

> the carceral, with its long gradation stretching from the convict

ship . . . to diffuse, slight limitations, communicates a type of power that the law validates and that justice uses as its favourite weapon . . . by means of a carceral continuum, the authority that sentences infiltrates all those other authorities that supervise, transform, correct, improve.

The apparent irrationality of the juvenile court, the unintended consequences of the complex interactions of the courtroom, fuses the projects of discipline and punishment. Thus meet sentencing and social structure.

However dubious, in a simple sense, the influence of the social inquiry report may be on sentencing, there is no doubt that the social inquiry stretches outwards from the courtroom in a far reaching way. For at the same time as magistrates exercise a relative autonomy in their generation of knowledge representations from the reports, their activities are none the less meaningless without reference to social work or more broadly to 'government through the family' (Donzelot 1980). While Donzelot's account refers to France, his basic analyses are eminently transferable to the UK context:

The question is not so much knowing what the family is used for in a liberal economy geared to private property as one of understanding why such a setup works, how the family came to constitute an effective way of warding off the dangers that hung over a liberal definition of the state when the poor revolted, demanding that it be made into the reorganizing principle of society . . . now what could have threatened a liberal definition of the state at the turn of the nineteenth century? . . . First . . . pauperism, the abrupt rise of those waves of indigents who . . . urged the [state] at the height of the Revolutionary period, to become the agency for . . . reorganizing the social body on the basis of the right of the poor to welfare, work and education. Secondly, the appearance of divisions with respect to living conditions and mores that ran so deep within the social body that they risked generating cataclysmic conflicts . . . a challenge to the very principle of a liberal society. The face to face encounter of a bourgeois minority and a barbarian populace that haunted the cities more than it inhabited them raised the spectre of their destruction

Donzelot 1980: 54

Philanthropy, argues Donzelot, emerged as a response to this problem, a 'Deliberately depoliticising strategy for establishing public services and facilities at a sensitive point midway between private initiative and the state (*ibid*: 55).

The success of the philanthropic strategy, crucially, derived from its preservation and transformation of the family, which became both a point of support for 'reabsorbing individuals for whom it had been inclined to relinquish responsibility' (*ibid*: 58) and a target, for 'by taking account of their complaints, they could be made agents for conveying the norms of the state into the private sphere' (*ibid*: 58). Through philanthropic assistance, morality was taken into the family, justifying a continuous surveillance into the details of family life. Particular attention was concentrated on the normalization of the adult–child relationship by philanthropists in whose 'Violent diatribes against the vagabondage of children these three elements are encountered . . . physical downfall . . . exploitation . . . and dangerousness (*ibid*: 79).

The 'tutelage formula' arose as a strategy to enforce the norms of petit bourgeois morality, centring around 'domestic hygiene' as a base for maintaining the social order (Joseph and Fritsch: 1977). The tutelary complex solved the problem of how to cope successfully with 'family resistances and individual deviations' in the working classes; it entailed government through, rather than of, the family: 'A wonderful mechanism since it enables the social body to deal with marginality through a near-total dispossession of private rights (*ibid*: 94). Virtually all the themes described by Donzelot appear in Elizabeth Gaskell's *Mary Barton*, published in 1848, and the crisis of order which the tutelary complex solved was explicitly commented on in her 'Preface':

> If it be an error that the woes, which come with an ever returning tide-like flood to overwhelm the workmen in our manufacturing towns, pass unregarded by all but the sufferers, it is . . . an error so bitter in its consequences to all parties, that whatever public effort can do in the way of legislation . . . should be done . . . the idea which I have formed of the state of feeling of among too many of the factory people in Manchester . . . has received some confirmation from the events which have so recently occurred among a similar class on the Continent.
>
> Gaskell 1970 (1848): 38

Responses to the threat of disorder in the UK were at least sufficiently comparable with the French context to lend a validity to Donzelot's analysis on both sides of the channel. Clearly developments stemming from specifically British economic and political conditions (for example the social themes of urbanization, industrialization, working-class militancy; cf. Morris and Giller 1987) shaped the form in which its own tutelary complex emerged; complex alignments of philanthropy, humanitarianism, hygiene and eugenics (cf. Garland 1981) within the political and economic formation must also be included in the history of the welfare sanction (cf. Parsloe 1978; Garland 1981; Morris and Giller 1987; Harris and Webb 1987). It is enough to note for present purposes that in England as well as in France the juvenile court became state as family ('an arrangement which recalls the oldest patriarchal rules' – Donzelot 1980: 104), a product of responses to crises of legitimacy under the conditions described by the philanthropists (cf. Gaskell 1970). Deprivation and depravation became linked through concepts of contamination/ corruption, poor living conditions being seen as 'both cause and effect of immorality and vice' (Worsley 1849, cited by Morris and Giller 1987). The working-class family was seen as 'ineffective, unreliable, and corrupting' (Morris and Giller 1987); the response was to enforce middle-class standards, 'respectable' standards, which 'marked the start of the state's promotion of desired family life and intervention to enforce it' (*ibid*: 22). Hence the introduction of the reformatories, often as 'preventive' measures for children in danger of 'contamination', a shift which involved the reformers in a concern with 'deviant character and lifestyle, with the immoral and the incorrigible' (*ibid*: 26).

And so, the 'juvenile court does not really pronounce judgement on crimes; it examines individuals' – although it might rather be said that the crimes upon which the juvenile court pronounces are as much violations of the norm as of the law and that it does not examine individuals, but cases (Foucault 1977). Clearly the social inquiry extends to link the family and the court via social work in a triad of surveillance, investigation and classification, the central techniques of 'government through the family'. Donzelot, however, emphasizes the lack of power of the judiciary in this relationship, seeing it as an 'accessory component of a control machinery'. In the UK context at least, this would be a mistake. For while magistrates need the social inquiry report as an instrument of surveillance, they operate in relative autonomy from it and themselves employ the social inquiry as a *method*, a way of seeing the relationship between offender and disposition. The juvenile court, while it is a *node* in the tutelary complex, also exercises a very real power of its own, in the application of knowledge to cases and the bifurcation of cases into hard and soft. It is an interorganizational arena where an uneasy alliance exists with the social work profession and where magistrates have their own status as agents of the tutelary complex. The latter is no more defined by psychiatry or social work than it is by the practices of the juvenile court alone.

The disciplinary practices of the juvenile court, carried out on the basis of the information mode of juvenile processing, reach out beyond the tutelary complex to a network of the carceral in general.

Moreover, the surveillance and classification enabled through the social inquiry thus links the juvenile court to every other disciplinary site: it at once implies them and draws upon them as a resource. The individual before the court is located within the carceral network and points of contact and dissonance are noted: army cadets, sea scouts, good YTS scheme . . .

> The whole pattern of the 'normal life' of young people, built around ideas of family socialization, profitable use of leisure, obedience and good progress at school, leading on to compliance in work discipline, and so on, has been called into question.
>
> Pratt 1983: 344

Thus the juvenile court through the social inquiry reaches out to the carceral network and seeks out the weaknesses in the child's links with it; then it seeks to mend weak or broken links with the limited resources at its disposal – the tariff. The carceral network, meanwhile, expands and reaches out hands to the juvenile court, ready to consign the 'failures' to its care. There is a basic fear of social disintegration implied by the attachment of magistrates to the idealized concept of the 'normal family' and a struggle against chaos which is implied by the impetus to classify and control reality according to the yardstick of familial 'normality'.

As the family is seen to 'fail' intervention is likely to increase. 'Normative law' means that the failure of the family to discipline and control can be seen as more serious than the offence itself. This is not a result of concern for the welfare of the offender, unless welfare is defined (as it was by some magistrates) as the level of discipline and control exercised over a child.

Youth is seen as something which, unbridled, is a powerful threat to society as a whole. The obsession with detailed social pathologies relates to the implied place of the child within the carceral network, within the family, within the community. Thus many offences were seen to emanate from 'awful enclosures' where 'all the families are bad', 'the offending is dreadful', 'high unemployment' – enclaves of disorder: 'I'm sure the local authority put them all together'. Young people from such areas, like Douglas's witches, beetles, and spiders,

> Attract the fears and dislikes which other ambiguities and contradictions attract in other thought structures; and the kind of powers attributed to them symbolise their ambiguous, inarticulate status.
>
> Douglas 1966: 104

Youth – especially the youth who are unemployed, the youth who pour out of the wainscoting, the public housing, at night to hang around street corners – represents a potential formlessness inhabiting the dark, obscure areas of society and so is seen to represent a threat. They represent a threat to no less than the authority of the community which magistrates as lay justices represent and have a duty to 'protect'.

Such youth has no obvious stake in the social order; it has no vote, no consumer power, no dependants, no mortgage, no property. Hence 'wandering around the streets' becomes a dangerous activity, the 'devil makes work for idle hands', and 'pollution dangers strike when form has been attacked' (Douglas 1966: 104). The maintenance of the (perceived) normative order, of discipline, of respect for private property, of moral 'decency', are threatened by the pollution of lower working-class youth and can only be sustained with the cooperation of the family, the employer, or the agencies of the state.

The threat of youth thus emanates from the social location of the judged, as viewed from the social location of the judges. The two locations are typically far apart and the 'knowledge' which magistrates have of that youth is unlikely to be based on experience of membership of the communities which they attempt to control (Bankowski and Mungham 1981). This very spatial and social distance creates the conditions for the mythological construction of the 'threat' of youth, as chronicled by Pearson (1983). Thus magistrates articulated 'respectable fears' and frequently contrasted present day disintegration with a golden past:

> There was depression in the thirties, but it didn't make us into criminals

> Things were different then, there was a real sense of community

> There has always been crime, we used to steal apples, but the local bobby gave you a good hiding and you didn't do it again.

> Discipline's gone out of the window these days.

Hence the concern for structured leisure, for parents 'knowing where their children are', for the exercise of patriarchal authority through the family, centres on a vision of the world 'as ought' which is under threat of siege.

Only the 'layness' of the magistracy explains this perspective on the 'other side' adequately. The 'world as ought' becomes 'the community' and 'the public' in the discourse of magistrates. 'The community expects' . . . Consequently a threat to the community is a threat to the magistracy (the custodians of the community) and vice versa. This kind of idealization is only a possibility because the magistracy is *not* grounded in the community: its legitimacy as a representative is as mythical as the 'normal family'. The community which it represents is a *notion*, and

> An ideologically based one, standing for different ways of organizing social life . . . its connotations of oneness and togetherness are often used to obfuscate the real divisions in society.
>
> Bankowski and Mungham 1981: 86

The 'interests of the child' and the 'interests of the public' come to be those which maintain the world of relative privilege and patronage occupied by the ' "acceptable" and "sensible" delegates from the "community" ' (*ibid*: 87) – a community of 'doing, belonging, leading people – who in any community must form a small though egregious minority' (Burney 1979: 73). The 'threat' of disorder posed by the judged to the judges, is a threat of all the other indisciplined young 'out there'. It is a threat which can only be understood with reference to their relative locations in the social structure: the one occupies an unknown dark terrain and the other a house of cards built on a mythical legitimacy.

A certain uneasiness may well be felt by those who occupy key positions in the well articulated sections of the social structure about the 'different dangers from its dark obscure areas' (Douglas 1966), since the magistracy has no democratic mandate, representing if anything only the interests of the carceral network itself.

The fear of disorder is thus ever present in the juvenile court: it is the fear of the margins experienced by those at the centre, and takes us full circle back to 1848. The juvenile justice system selects representatives who are made to stand proxy for all the uncountable beetles in the wainscoting; it then classifies them in relation to the 'normative order'. Perhaps after all, the tutelary complex did not solve the problem of order, and knowledge is not power but only a frenetic attempt to sustain power. The classification of juveniles represents the attempt to control reality by pinning it down. But if the whole naming process is an attempt to gloss over some underlying rupture, then perhaps all the effort to 'tame', to classify, to describe, is perpetually under threat.

> Sanity is the ability to appreciate reality. The rock is solid. It goes down and joins the floors of the sea and that is joined to the floors I have known. I must remember that the rock is solid and immoveable. If the rock were to move then I should be mad.
>
> A flying lizard flapped overhead, then dropped down out of sight.
>
> Golding 1979: 163

CHAPTER 9

The future of the
social inquiry

One of the things that has happened to us in the twentieth century . . . is to learn how certainty crumbles in your hand.

Salman Rushdie 14 February 1990

At the symbolic level, then, lawlessness invokes the terror of doubt; a dark, disordered world out there which threatens the sacred. Whether the sacred is enshrined in religion, in property, in human life, it represents that which is absolute, or more precisely, that which social groupings deeply desire to uphold as absolute. Those who speak in the name of the sacred are the agents through whom upright consciences are 'brought together and concentrated' (Durkheim 1964).

The magistrates interviewed in this study on the whole perceived themselves as representatives of the upright conscience. For many of them, the crumbling certainty of the twentieth century was felt to be a threat, represented in part by the flow of unruly and undisciplined youth through their courts. Their duty as they saw it was to make the best of a virtually impossible task, to try through their 'limited' powers to inject at least enough moral fibre into the lives of the families before them to provide some hope of salvation. If salvation was not seen as possible then only retribution remained.

Thus magistrates acted and reacted within the complex domain of the juvenile court, becoming practised in the routinized strategies of courtroom culture, producing and reproducing the structures of justice. Within this site, at once home to local and specific discourses and practices, yet reaching along a global continuum, the techniques of power we have called the social inquiry were framed and deployed.

Precisely because the minutiae of everyday practice are intimately linked to the wider enterprise of social control, practitioners responsible for social information provision need to take account of the 'big issues' in the delivery of justice. The provision of social data to the juvenile court in the form of social inquiry reports thus occupies a central position in the social relations of juvenile justice. This centrality, however, is contradictory. Social inquiry reports, reflecting the position of social work generally in relation to the courts, tend to assist in the spectacle of justice. Rather than commanding an audience they tend to respond to an agenda set by punitiveness. The social inquiry report becomes part of a process of multiple displacement whereby the individual who has committed an offence successively becomes a case.

A series of blocks are set up to communication. Reports interpret the offender to the magistrates, who reinterpret the reinterpretation; solicitors also reinterpret the report and magistrates reinterpret their reinterpretation. The real voice of the offender, the voice of the victim and the voices of those surrounding them in their socal milieux are progressively silenced through the processes of reporting and the bureaucratic practices of the juvenile court. The complexities of offending behaviour, of the problems of the families involved, are almost inevitably represented in a scaled up, scaled down, homogenized form (Law 1986). These problems are at once presented as more and less than their reality as experienced by those directly involved. They are lost in the classificatory conventions as the 'cascades of intermediaries' (Callon 1986) are interposed between the 'masses' and their spokesmen.

This has practical implications for the provision of social information to the court. Hitherto the debate surrounding the appropriate content and format of social inquiry reports has been carried out without reference to any detailed empirical knowledge of the way in which such information would be interpreted by magistrates. The current study suggests that the point made by Tutt and Giller in 1984 needs reinforcement: 'Social inquiry reports are written for courts to determine what should happen to an offender as the consequence of the commission of a proved offence' (Tutt and Giller 1984) and they should thus be 'focused documents with a specific purpose for a limited exercise' (*ibid*).

There has, in the aftermath of the welfare/justice controversy, been a tendency towards attempting to rescue the social work approach to criminal justice. This has involved taking into account the points made by the 'back to justice' (Morris *et al.* 1980) lobby but reiterating the value of a commitment to 'caring' (Hudson 1987; Bottoms and Stelman 1989). Bottoms and Stelman, for example, contend that a 'balanced' view of SIR practice needs to reflect 'social work knowledge and experience, social work skills, and social work values' (*ibid*: 39). There is, they argue, a need not only to remember who reports are written *for* but also who they are written *by*. The problem with this proposition (leaving aside the question of the desirability of the application of social work values to offenders and their families) is that any consideration of social information independently of the context into which it is sent will probably reinforce the modes of punitive sentencing highlighted in the present study. Social work discourse is likely to be reappropriated in the court setting according to the routine modes of operating and the interpretative conventions of magistrates which already exist in the juvenile court. Most importantly, magistrates were found to interpret so called 'welfare' categories in terms of potentiality for discipline and control.

The only exception to this would be if such a report-writing strategy had been negotiated and agreed in advance between the bench and agency at local level and if the nature of existing court practice had been tackled. For reasons which will be further discussed below, this is unlikely (though not impossible) in most areas.

A selective rehabilitation of Streatfeild (Bottoms and Stelman) is thus likely to provide sentencers with further sources from which to manufacture images of control and discipline and to strengthen the practices of normative sentencing. Hence there is a problem with conducting practice debates in terms of what is 'desirable'. The empirical question of the likely impact of practices has to be addressed. While social work as a profession may (although it may not) wish to challenge the existing mode of youth justice, an adherence to report-writing practices based around social work values may well result in inappropriate use of SIR data, in continuing confusion among magistrates as to the appropriate use of such data and in the continuing misrepresentation of working-class lives as selective biographies which are both tactically dangerous and patronizing.

Nor does the approach suggested by Pratt (1985) help a great deal in this respect. Pratt suggests that report writers adopt a 'naturalistic' rather than a 'positivistic' approach to their raw material; an 'accurate reconstruction' (*ibid*: 15) rather than an attempted 'explanation'. It is, of course, impossible to let the data 'speak for themselves', as this study has attempted to show. The very acts of selection and ordering impose an implicit ordering on the data. The interpretation of offending offered by the report would thus go underground, leaving even more to the interpretative creativity of the report readers. Magistrates, indeed, have acute problems in understanding *direct* communication from defendants and their families; particularly with their vocabularies of motive. It is unlikely that they would have more success with a social worker's naturalistic 'summary' of such frames of meaning! Such reports would be even more amenable to an unfavourable reconstruction by sentencers (*Report*: 'Bill says he just took the jacket because it was there and he had wanted one for a while. He was bored and thought it would be a good laugh. Unemployment is high in this area and opportunities for Bill to get a Saturday job to buy his own jacket are limited.' *Magistrate*: 'A shocking case. Lots of people are unemployed and they don't go around stealing things other people have worked for. If that's his attitude he had better get representation'.) The only helpful form of 'naturalism' would be to involve the defendant and his or her family more fully and equally in the process of communicating with sentencers and in promoting a fuller understanding of their lives by sentencers. This is unlikely to happen in the context of a social work report.

These sadly negative points are further reinforced when magistrates' existing perceptions and practices are considered in relation to current legislative developments in youth control, in particular the 1989 Children's Act and the 1990 White Paper *Crime, Justice and Protecting the Public* (HMSO 1990). For while there can be no simple conflation of policy and practice, the 1989 Act and the White Paper will tend to reinforce rather than challenge the existing culture and structure of social information use as presented in this study.

Magistrates are, of course, unlikely to swallow wholesale the proposals contained in these documents – they are likely to resist attempts to curtail their custodial sentencing (Parker, Sumner and Jarvis 1989) and have shown a reluctance to use their powers to impose night curfews or to bind over parents of juvenile defendants (probably because they are aware of the impracticalities of these measures, as acknowledged in the White Paper). In general terms, however, the current and proposed legislation encourages and legitimates the use of a socialized tariff based on control indicators in juvenile cases. 'Just desserts' may be the predominant message, but it is a message of proportionality in relation to *lives* and not simply to *acts* which is at issue. If parental supervision and control is to be placed officially at the heart of the sentencing process for juveniles, then it is no more or less than a ratification of the mode of sentencing found to be operating by this study in 1985–88. The simplicity of the just desserts with mitigation model is always already infused with a judgement of the social background of offenders, their location within the disciplinary networks; to this extent, policy seems to have followed practice. Thus the following extract from the White Paper could have been a tape transcript from interviews with any number of the magistrates who gave their views in the current study:

> Parents should know where their children are and what they are doing, and be in a position to exercise some supervision over them . . . the criminal law has a part to play in making parents as well as children face up to their responsibilities . . .
>
> HMSO 1990

Where legislative principle legitimates existing practice a powerful amalgam is the result. The magistracy may well come into conflicts with significant aspects of the 1989 Act and the White Paper but the developing legislative framework can be selectively appropriated and integrated with the existing culture and structure of justice. Attempts to erode magisterial discretion produce resistances, but these are creative resistances which will utilize the new directions in terms of existing local practices. The development of 'control sentencing', the creation of a 'youth court' dealing exclusively with criminal cases, is likely to further strengthen existing tendencies.

The most recent guidance to report writers in juvenile cases was set out in the DHSS publication *Reports to Courts*. This document emphasizes that the primary focus of reports should be on offending, with detailed comment on the current offence, and an avoidance of the 'routine parading' of 'irrelevant and unconnected' information. On family background, however, the document comments:

> (Family) background will be required where it serves to explain the circumstances of the offence, or where it relates to the appropriateness of the various options open to the court.
>
> DHSS 1987

Clearly, taken within the context of current legislative developments, this would imply that data relating to the level of parental supervision and control, the ability of parents to effect control and their willingness to cooperate with intervention, becomes relevant. The inclusion of generic family background information in reports would be more likely to be interpreted in this light than in any version of social work values of 'caring'. This is further reinforced by the stereotyping of family life and of the relationship of family life to offending which is currently prevalent in the wider social discourses of media and political rhetoric. Recent key statements by Kenneth Baker and by Margaret Thatcher, for example, have repeatedly thrown the 'evils' of single parenthood and working mothers into the limelight as 'threats' to the social fabric (*The Guardian* 7 May 1990, 19 May 1990; *The Today Programme*, BBC Radio Four, 14 May 1990).

The social inquiry report may function to place the offending behaviour in context, but it can have little effectiveness in promoting the understanding of offending behaviour in a wider sense. The climate in which such an understanding could be reached would have to pre-exist the report, implying a wider awareness and flexibility, and a greater readiness to accept a critical analysis of society, than currently exist among the magistracy, the police or the politicians (Harwin 1982). The fostering of such a climate begins not with the individual report writer, but at the 'organizational and system' level (Tutt and Giller 1984). As it is, certain strong assumptions about the 'causes' of offending already underly the operation of the juvenile justice system: offending behaviour stems from a breakdown in parental supervision, from individual irresponsibility, from lack of discipline. In this context the functions of the report must necessarily be limited and it may be that some of the most useful strategies to be adopted by report writers will be a development of the practice of 'leaving out' rather than 'including in' much social background information, as Tutt and Giller's approach suggests. These practices have of course begun to be developed in some areas, particularly by the probation service, (Bottoms and Stelman 1989) through an increased emphasis on focused and offence specific report writing and an emphasis on selectivity in the provision of reports.

Four underpinning propositions are therefore suggested as the bases for report-writing practice:

1 Report-writing practice should be aimed at securing minimal intervention in the vast majority of juvenile cases, for the very good reasons that this is likely to prove the best way of preventing the development of an 'offending career' (Tutt and Giller 1984; DHSS 1987).
2 Report-writing practice should *avoid* addressing generalized welfare needs because they are likely to be inappropriately utilized as indicators of the strength of social integration, supervision and discipline to which the offender is subject generally in his or her life (thus encouraging the judgement of lives rather than acts). If positive help with problems as perceived by the young person or his or her family is *wanted*, then that should be offered outside the framework of a report which is being prepared for a criminal court in relation to specific offences.
3 Report-writing practice should avoid intruding into the lives of offenders and their families and the consequent imposition of the techniques of 'hierarchical surveillance' and 'normalizing judgements' by middle-class social workers: it should have nothing to do with 'lifting up the lids of cooking pots' (Donzelot 1980). The offender and his or her family has a right to privacy and autonomy in the conduct of their lives which should only be questioned under very extreme circumstances.
4 Report-writing practice should recognize that the legitimate concerns of the juvenile court – particularly with the impending segregation of the family and youth courts – are limited to the issues relating specifically to the offences under consideration at any one time.

The implications of report content stemming from these propositions are fairly obvious. Information relating to family background would be included *only* where it has direct situational relevance to the specific instances of offending behaviour under consideration at a particular court appearance. This goes further than the DHSS guidelines in that it implies that family background is only relevant where it can be included under a discussion of the immediate circumstances of the offence. An example of this might be where a young person, after a disagreement with his or her parents, walks out of the family home, sleeps rough and commits offences in this situation. In other words, we are talking here of directly precipitating circumstances. Even in such a case as this, it would be wiser to avoid an overly extensive account of relationships within the family. 'Explaining offending' is thus limited to a consideration of specific events which make the actions of the offender more comprehensible, *not* a general analysis of the family dynamics.

A further justification for including family background data might be where a specific supervisory package is being recommended and where *positive* reasons can be found from a discussion with the family to suppose that the package would be a useful intervention. Consistently with the proposition of minimal intervention, such a package would only be offered to offenders at high risk of custody and a report would avoid any routine allusion to negative indicators *against* supervision packages from the family background – if supervision is not being offered, then there is no reason to use negative familial control indicators to justify this decision.

Excepting within the context of the circumstances of the offence or supporting supervision, family background would not be discussed in the report. Positively, the report may provide a realistic and non-rhetorical assessment of the degree of social harm caused by an offence. Frequently the degree of social harm resulting from juvenile offences is small, if it is separated from the symbolic fear of lawlessness. The report could instil a sense of proportion in considering the offence; to acknowledge pain when it is inflicted but to underline the largely nuisance nature of many offences.

The report may also reintroduce the victim. In many cases there is no reason to assume that the best interests of the victim will be served by custodial or high intervention disposals. The victim's perception of the offence, too, may not be that which magistrates would assume, particularly if mediation or reparation is seen as possible.

Continual reinforcement that high intervention disposals are in many cases inappropriate is a message that should be made clear in the content of reports; at the agency level, indeed, this may be most effectively achieved by ensuring that reports are only provided in cases where they are requested or where the offender is thought to be at risk of custody. This means reserving report writing for the heavy end, extending the policy which many areas have now adopted of not routinely providing reports on first offenders to not routinely providing reports on any but the most serious offenders.

Finally, the report should address specific criteria relating to the use of custody and alternatives to custody, if it is thought that custody is at issue. Reports should attempt to ensure that sentencers consider the criteria laid out in s. 1(4) of the 1982 Criminal Justice Act and amended by the 1988 Criminal Justice Act. Report writers should ensure that they have provided sentencers with all the information in their power to enable the criteria to be stringently applied.

Further questions will be raised for future report-writing practice if increasing use is made by sentencers of powers to bind parents over or to attach night curfews to supervision orders, or if residence requirements for supervision orders become popular with magistrates. The whole stress in the Children Act and the White Paper on supervision and control by parents of children may come to pose difficulties for report writers, who could be pressured by magistrates in to providing exactly the kind of 'control' information it is suggested here should be excluded from report-writing practice. In this event report writers could only take the line of providing as specific information as possible on parental supervision and control. This might involve obtaining a specific statement from parents themselves about, for example, their commitment to supervision, rather than a social worker's assessment of the 'level of supervision in the home'.

The role of school reports must be seen, if anything, as even more problematic given the findings of the present study and that of Parker *et al.* (1989). Magistrates look to school reports as indicators of the degree of a child's incorrigibility, while at the same time agreeing that such reports are often negative, value laden and selective. The introduction of new legislation (for example, the concept of an education supervision order) suggests a radical rethink of the whole approach to the provision of school based information. The first step must be to confront and educate the teaching profession in the preparation of information for the court and in the need to provide a positive view of the child's capabilities and behaviour. In relation to criminal offences it seems that unless the school setting is directly related to the circumstances of the offences under consideration, then a school report should simply not be provided – alternatively, as Sumner *et al.* (1988) suggest, *relevant* school based information could be provided within the social inquiry report.

If such suggestions as these seem hopelessly restrictive in terms of offering positive social work intervention or in terms of educating the bench into a more enlightened approach towards young offenders, it is because such debates cannot be pursued at the level of report-writing practice. As Tutt and Giller (1984) have correctly observed, achievements must be limited unless the social information question is first tackled at the level of the organization and the system. Wider change implies more effective communication – in terms of engaged debate, not superficial liaison – between local agencies and the juvenile panel; and the development of a wider ranging debate around issues of youth control at national level.

Through debate at a local level agencies have their best opportunity to negotiate with the bench and to affect its informal policies in dealing with juvenile offenders. Of the six court areas studied, only in court B had agencies made a concerted attempt to enter into a dialogue with the bench and the clerk and to draw key members of the bench into a consideration of the broader issues relating to offending, in particular in relation to the need for low intervention and an avoidance of custodial sentencing. It would be impossible for individual social workers or probation officers to adopt the kinds of principles and strategies suggested above without support at the level of agency policy. It would be equally unlikely for such principles and strategies to succeed in challenging bench practices if effected only at the level of report-writing changes. As has been argued previously, the report is the weak link for agencies; it is sent into a complex environment and can be challenged from many directions in its attempts to 'articulate conceptions about the world and to impose them on others'.

It is at the level of bench–agency relations that the context into which reports are going to be received must be addressed. Through bench–agency contact (both formal and informal) communication, debate and an honest acknowledgement of the limits to which co-operation can extend may at least be established. The chances of less punitive and control oriented reported writing being accepted by the bench are greater if:

1 Key members of the bench can be 'recruited' to take an active interest in progressive local initiatives in juvenile justice such as IIT projects, mediation schemes etc.
2 An understanding of the problems experienced by local communities can be encouraged, so that offending is seen as only one issue in relation to a number of others which may be being addressed by local groups (such as unemployment, lack of leisure facilities, public amenities).

3 The bench are made aware of the benefits of low intervention and other initiatives such as diversion, mediation and reparation and agencies ensure that magistrates understand the aims and operation of these resources, especially where they are available locally.

Realistically, of course, the obstacles to achieving a high degree of cooperation on low intervention and to achieving the degree of communication necessary to this strategy are great, as the present research perhaps shows only too clearly. But agencies would at least have established a clear policy based on challenging bifurcatory sentencing; they would have made explicit what reports were intended to achieve; and both sides would be left with a recognition of where they stood and the limits of possible cooperation.

Clearly, however, because of the deliberate semi-compatibility of these proposals with the existing juvenile justice system, the concept of the limited reform implies an ultimate inadequacy. While the localized nature of the court system allows potential for changes in the nature of report provision and a limited amount of cooperation between bench and agencies, sooner or later one encounters the broader political issues which began this chapter. The links between juvenile justice policies and the current political and economic issues confronting the Conservative state, and with the more enduring issues of justice within a capitalist society, justify the contention that a far more radical restructuring of juvenile justice is necessary if the social inquiry is to become a means of effective communication rather than a technique of power.

Strategies for achieving juvenile justice are needed which promote the *understanding* of offending behaviour by, first, preserving the autonomy and rationality of individual action but equally locating that action within structural constraints. This is based not on the pathological approach of 'diagnosing' offending as if it were an illness, but viewing it sociologically as the result of the interaction between agency and structure. This is related to Box's concept of a demand for justice:

A demand for justice . . . has to include a demand for *understanding* the offender. It needs this not in the hope that the offender will then be condoned, excused or justified. Nor does understanding necessarily shift the blame back onto the victim. The demand for understanding is necessary because although people choose to act, sometimes criminally, they *do not do so under conditions of their own choosing*. Their choice makes them responsible, but the conditions of their choice make the choice comprehensible. These conditions, social and economic, contribute to crime because they constrain, limit or narrow the choices available . . .

Box 1987: 29 (original emphases)

Social information as communication is only fully possible when information ceases to be part of the knowledge/power enterprise: this implies far reaching changes in the organization of juvenile justice. 'Better' reports and 'better' bench–agency relations are only worthwhile if they are conceived of as transitional strategies which would be accompanied by parallel strategies aimed at wider change. Without such wider change, the organizational structure of the courtroom still exists; the 'control and punish' orientation of the magistracy still exists; the juvenile court, in short, still exists as an inherently disciplinarian and punitive institution.

These histories cannot be decided by any lone commentator; but it *can* reasonably be suggested that report-writing practices should take a minimalist approach and that reports should be strategically limited and focused towards their necessarily narrow role as far as the present state of juvenile justice is concerned.

It is not the role of the researcher/commentator to dictate practice issues; and in this sense the above discussion is offered only as a set of propositions for debate which are consistent with the findings of this study of magistrates at work. To the extent that a reconsideration of social information requires the asymmetries of power within the social relations of juvenile justice to be addressed, these propositions are inevitably limited. History cannot be written in advance; and only tiny fragments of the present can be repositioned without needing to re-compose the whole. The practitioners who are directly involved in producing the history of the justice system need also to examine carefully the positioning of the fragments with which they daily work. This book is intended as just one of many possible interventions in that process.

APPENDIX 1

Research design

The research design was implemented in three stages:

Phase 1: Initial observation of juvenile court hearings; informal discussions with participants; analysis of documentary sources of information.

Phase 2: Design and testing of observation and interview methods; further observation of court hearings, initial interviews with clerks to the justices and magistrates using these methods.

Phase 3: Selection of courts for the main research; dimensions of selection: socioeconomic and court characteristics (see Appendix 2); access negotiations.

The original research design contained a fourth phase which involved following through a sample of specific cases systematically and in detail. This phase was never fully implemented, for reasons which are discussed briefly below (see also Brown 1989).

Initial local contacts available through colleagues in the Department of Administrative and Social Studies, Teesside Polytechnic, were used for phase 1 of the research design outlined above. Access was gained to two courts for observation. During this period, involving ten observation sessions and ten unstructured taped interviews, the form of the observation and interview schedules was developed. Meanwhile contacts were being established with courts and agencies in other regions with a view to gaining access for the main phases of the research.

Observation schedules

Two methods of recording observation sessions were decided upon: a fairly structured instrument for recording information events and contextual field notes for setting these within the broader institutional practice of the court.

The semi-structured schedule aimed to divide interaction into information events or exchanges, recording each exchange of social information representations along the following dimensions:

- source (where did the message come from);
- direction (to whom was it directed);
- nature of interaction (face to face, one to one, were documents involved, etc.);
- manner of message delivery (interrogative, admonitory, routine informative);
- duration of message;
- content of message (verbatim as far as possible);
- context of message (prosecution account, defence mitigation, sentencing 'homily' etc.).

The schedule also routinely recorded the offence for which the defendant was being sentenced; case numbers for co-defendants if applicable (separate sheets were completed for each defendant even where several were being sentenced together); whether the offence had been admitted or found proved; sentencing outcome; whether reports were available; and the personnel present during the hearing (e.g. parents, social worker etc.) including whether or not the defendant was represented by a solicitor. Except for the 'content' of the message these were completed by ringing symbols or brief notation in a matter of seconds. Each schedule thus covered one defendant being sentenced for one or more offences and recorded all exchanges during the sentencing process where social information representations were invoked and deployed.

Because the observation schedule dealt only with the formal aspects of social information deployment, field notebooks were also maintained. These were used to record broader contexts; observations on the organizational processes of the court, informal interactions and conversations, and potentially significant aspects of the proceedings which were not immediately related to social information exchanges.

The aim was to record on the schedules every case which proceeded to disposition, providing that the defendant was aged 14 years or over and a social inquiry report has been requested.

Interview schedules

The nature of the interviews with magistrates have been discussed in some detail in Chapter 1. In fact schedule is something of a misnomer for what actually emerged for use in interviewing magistrates. Using the shopping list of substantive topics outlined in Chapter 1 and the methods described there of broadening out to contexts of statements, the interviews took the following form.

Introductions and general talk was followed by a brief description of the research project. The structuring device of substantive topics was used as a fall back to ensure that each substantive area had been raised as a topic with each respondent, but in practice it was rarely needed as the topics listed there almost always arose naturally during the course of the conversation/ interview. For example, an interview might begin along the following lines:

(I = interviewer, R = respondent)

I: We are trying to look at social information and sentencing from the magistrates' point of view. Trying to get a 'magistrates' eye' view, if you like . . . So really, what I'd like, is your own personal account of whether you feel that social information is important in sentencing juveniles, you know . . . what sort of information is useful, and really, how it fits into your job as a sentencer . . .

R: I see . . . are you just looking at the social report, things like that?

I: No. The social inquiry report does come into it, but really we're interested in social information in general, whether it comes from the social inquiry report or somewhere else.

R: Because you can tell sometimes you know just from having them in front of you. Or you can look down the court list and certain names, certain areas, well!

I: How does that help, having them in front of you?

R: Well, it's the way they look at you, how they are. I don't mean their clothes, you've got to be very careful about that . . . it's their whole . . . attitude to you. You can tell an awful lot. Sometimes you can tell they're really sorry, they're ashamed, but others! . . .

I: How useful is that kind of 'direct' information, do you think, compared with the social inquiry report?

R: It's more that you are trying to piece it all together really. You are trying to get an overall picture of the child, and the social inquiry report comes into it. It's the whole child you're trying to get at.

I: When you say a picture, what kind of picture is it you're after, what do you want to know about . . .

R: Yes, yes. It's what makes them tick really, you're trying to . . . for instance the family background. It's the first thing . . . Because so much of it's to do with broken homes, they've no father or their father's not a real father, so they've never had any proper guidance . . . so it's not surprising when they end up in court, but you want to know, whether there's anything to build on in the home background . . .

I: To build on?

R: Yes, what is the control like in the home, does he have any real interests, do they know where he is when he goes out . . .

I: How might that actually help you?

R: Well, oh, it's difficult without a case in front of me. Like this morning, the boy you saw . . .

The interviewer thus attempted to continually broaden out discussion and home in on specific questions, telescoping in and out of issues from the case specific to the global – from, say, a detailed discussion of a case which had been before the court the morning of the interview, to general attitudes to offending and youth, perhaps back in again to a discussion of the difficulties of the magistrate's job and so on.

Characteristics of court areas and samples

Because of resource constraints, the courts selected were within the north and north-east of England, but varied in:

1 demographic composition of the area served;
2 sentencing patterns;
3 size of panel and number of cases processed.

The initial approach was made through the clerk to the justices, and the local social services/probation service were also contacted. In some areas the latter were also instrumental in helping to negotiate access. The agencies in each area were also approached with a view to gaining access to social inquiry reports.

Sixteen courts were approached, of which six ultimately materialized as research sites. These are referred to as courts A to F within the text; their characteristics are briefly described in Table 1.

Table 1 Demographic composition of areas served.

Unemployment

Court	Sub-region	% unemployed (October 84)
A	A	23
B	B	19
C	C	10
D	C	10
E	D	20
F	E	17

(sub-region C covers courts C and D)

Population density

Court	Sub-region	Persons per sq. km.
A	A	969
B	B	249
C	C	82
D	C	82
E	D	2121
F	E	840

Social class

Court	Sub-region	% with head of household in:		
		I/II	III	IV/V
A	A	17	38	21
B	B	17	37	19
C	C	28	32	15
D	as C			
E	D	16	38	18
F	E	16	40	18

General characteristics of court areas

A   Declined industrial town, high unemployment
B   City, non-metropolitan
C   City, non-metropolitan
D   Town, rural area, tourism dominated
E   Metropolitan area
F   Metropolitan area

Sentencing patterns: see Appendix 2.

Magistrates interviewed in each court area

Table 2   Magistrates interviewed.

Court	Juvenile panel size	Number interviewed	% of panel
A	32	14	42 S
B	18	13	72 P
C	21	17	81 P
D	16	13	81 P
E	39	17	44 S
F	54	18	33 S

See Table 2. In courts A, E and F a sample only (S) of the panel was selected at the request of the clerk to the justices. In the case of courts E and F this was for administrative reasons and a random sample was taken of 50 per cent for court E and 33 per cent for court F. The response rates for these courts were thus 88 per cent and 100 per cent respectively although as a proportion of the panel as a whole they represented 44 per cent and 33 per cent respectively. In the remaining courts the whole panel was approached (P). Court A was a special case in that the sample was selected by the clerk and was non-random. The results may therefore be seen as fairly representative of the panel's views except in the case of court A where some bias inevitably occurred and the nature of that bias cannot be known.

Observation periods

During the observation periods courts would be attended at roughly fortnightly intervals, so that for, example, 13 observation sessions would cover approximately a six-month period. Thus temporary peculiarities in the intake of cases should not have affected the observation unduly. The observation period extended from the end of 1985 to the end of 1988. More observation data was collected from courts A and E than from other courts and while every effort has been made not to over-emphasize material from these courts, it is likely that some bias has been inevitable. A low throughput for courts B and D combined with less observation input mean that the number of cases observed was less than would have been desirable.

Social inquiry reports

122 SIRs from court areas A–E were examined. The analysis of SIRs is biased towards courts A and E, for which it was possible to obtain a set of reports for the period studied. Court B agencies required the agreement of the client, which made reports difficult to obtain; in court C, social services reports could be obtained by following up the authors; in court D, reports could be obtained by informal negotiation with the court officer. Due to time constraints reports relating to court F were not obtained. Thus 92 of the reports examined originated from court areas A and E.

APPENDIX 2

Sentencing outcomes by court area

Key to abbreviations used in Figures 1–11

AD/CD Absolute/conditional discharge
AC   Attendance centre order
SO   Supervision order
CSO   Community service order
DC   Detention centre
YC   Youth custody

The figures show the percentage of offenders in a particular age/sex grouping receiving a particular disposition out of all those sentenced for indictable offences for that age/sex grouping during the year indicated. 'Total sentenced' thus equals 100 per cent within the sex and age group defined. For example, if court X sentenced 100 boys aged 14–17 during 1986 and 35 received fines, then the percentage shown as 'fine' on the graph would be 35.

The figures given relate to the year in which fieldwork was undertaken for that court, except in the case of court F, where fieldwork was undertaken in 1988 but the figures relate to 1987 (1988 criminal statistics not available at time of writing). England and Wales percentages are given for 1986 and 1987.

Figure 1   Court A sentencing outcomes 1986: males aged 14–17

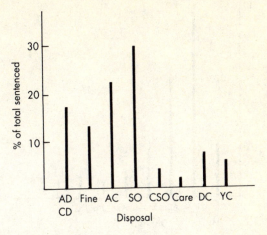

Source: Home Office (1988b)

Figure 2   Court B: sentencing outcomes 1986: males aged 14–17

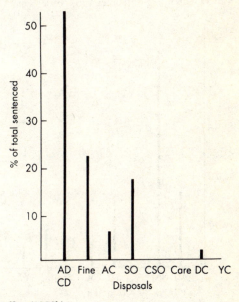

Source: Home Office (1988b)

Figure 3   Court C: sentencing outcomes 1987: males aged 14–17

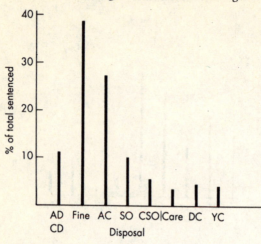

Source: Home Office (1988b)

Figure 4   Court D sentencing outcomes 1987: males aged 14–17

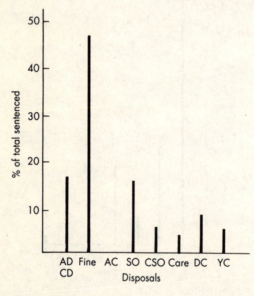

Source: Home Office (1988b)

Figure 5   Court E sentencing outcomes 1986: males aged 14–17

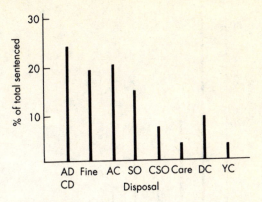

Source: Home Office (1988b)

Figure 6   Court F sentencing outcomes 1987: males aged 14–17

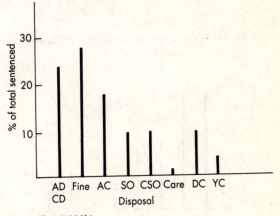

Source: Home Office (1988b)

Figure 7   Court F sentencing outcomes 1987: females aged 14–17[a]

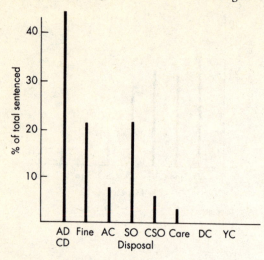

Source: Home Office (1988b)

[a] In all other courts the throughput of females was too low to allow for valid representation in percentage breakdowns.

Figure 8   England and Wales sentencing outcomes 1986: males aged 14–17

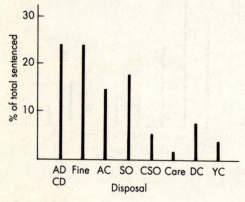

Source: Home Office (1988a)

Figure 9   England and Wales sentencing outcomes 1987: males aged 14–17

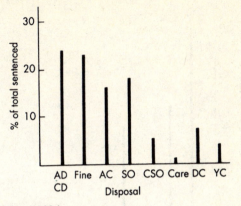

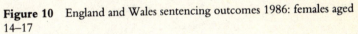

Source: Home Office (1988a)

Figure 10   England and Wales sentencing outcomes 1986: females aged 14–17

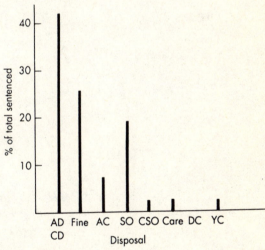

Source: Home Office (1988a)

Figure 11   England and Wales sentencing outcomes 1987: females aged 14–17

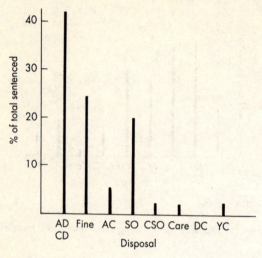

Source: Home Office (1988a)

Bibliography

Abrams, P. (ed.) (1981). *Practice and Progress: British Sociology 1950–1980*. London, Allen & Unwin.

Aldrich, H. (1971). 'Organizational boundaries and interorganizational conflict', *Human Relations*, 24, 279–93.

Althusser, L. (1969). 'Ideology and the State' in *Lenin and Philosophy and Other Essays*. London, Allen Lane.

Asquith, S. (1983). *Children and Justice*. Edinburgh, Edinburgh University Press.

Baden-Powell, R. (1930). *Rovering to Success: A Book of Life Sport for Young Men*. London, Herbert Jenkins.

Ball, C. (1983). 'Secret justice: the use made of school reports in the juvenile court', *British Journal of Social Work*, 13, 197–206.

Bankston, W.B. (1983). 'Legal and extra legal offender traits and decision making in the criminal justice system', *Sociological Spectrum*, 3 (1), 1–18.

Bankowski, Z. and Mungham, G. (1981). 'Lawpeople and laypeople', *International Journal of the Sociology of Law*, 9, 85–100.

Bankowski, Z.D. *et al.* (1987). *Lay Justice?* Edinburgh: T. & T. Clark.

Barnes, B. (1977). *Interests and the Growth of Knowledge*. London, Routledge & Kegan Paul.

Barnes, B. (1988). *The Nature of Power*. Oxford, Polity/Basil Blackwell.

Bean, P. (1971). 'The challenge of social enquiry reports', *Family Law*, 1 (6), 174–8.

Bean, P. (1985). 'Social enquiry reports: a recommendation for disposal', *Justice of the Peace*, 139, 568–9 and 585–7.

Benbasat, I. and Taylor, R.N. (1982). 'Behavioral aspects of information processing for the design of management information systems', *IEEE Transactions on Systems: Man and Cybernetics SMC*, 12, 439–50.

Benson, J.K. (1975). 'The interorganizational network as a political economy', *Administrative Science Quarterly*, 20, 229–49.

Berger, J. (1972). *Ways of Seeing*. Harmondsworth, Penguin.

Bittner, E. (1974). 'The concept of organisation' in R. Turner (ed.), *Ethno-methodology*. Harmondsworth, Penguin.

Bottoms, A.E. (1983). 'Some neglected features of contemporary penal systems' in D. Garland and P. Young (eds), *The Power to Punish: Contemporary Penality and Social Analysis*. London, Heinemann.

Bottoms, A.E. and McWilliams, W. (1986). 'Social inquiry reports twenty-five years after the Streatfeild Report' in P. Bean and D. Whynes (eds), *Barbara Wotton, Social Science and Public Policy: Essays in their Honour*. London, Tavistock.

Bottoms, A.E. and Stelman, A. (1989). *Social Inquiry Reports*. Aldershot, Gower.

Bourdieu, P. (1984). *Distinction*. London, Routledge & Kegan Paul.

Box, S. (1986). 'Crime and punishment', *Unemployment Unit Bulletin Issue* 19, February.

Box, S. (1987). *Recession, Crime and Punishment*. London, Macmillan.

Bradden, E. (1983). 'Survey of youngsters sentenced to a detention centre during 1980', *Clearing House for Social Services Research*, 9, December, 55–89.

Brown, S. (1989). *Social Information and Its 'Usefulness' in the Juvenile Court: An Analysis of Magistrates' Accounts in Organizational Context*. Ph.D. thesis, Teesside Polytechnic Department of Administrative and Social Studies, July 1989.

Burney, E. (1979). *Magistrate, Court and Community*. London, Heinemann.

Burton, F. and Carlen, P. (1979). *Official Discourse*. London, Routledge & Kegan Paul.

Butler, I. (1983). 'Some implications for social work practice' in J. Lishman, *Research Highlights 5: Social Work with Adult Offenders*. University of Aberdeen, Department of Social Work.

Cain, M. and Finch, J. (1981). 'Towards a rehabilitation of data' in P. Abrams (ed.), *Practice and Progress: British Sociology 1950–1980*. London, Allen and Unwin.

Callon, M. (1986). 'Some elements of a sociology of translation: domestication of scallops and the fishermen of St Brieuc Bay' in J. Law (ed.), *Power, Action, and Belief: A New Sociology of Knowledge? Sociological Review. Monograph 32*, University of Keele/Routledge & Kegan Paul.

Carlen, P. (1976). *Magistrates' Justice*. Oxford, Martin Robertson.

Carlen, P. (1983a). *Women's Imprisonment: A Study in Social Control*. London, Routledge & Kegan Paul.

Carlen, P. (1983b). 'On rights and powers: some notes on penal politics' in D. Garland and P. Young (eds), *The Power to Punish: Contemporary Penality and Social Analysis*, London, Heinemann.

Carter, R.M. (1967). 'The presentence report and the decision making process', *Journal of Research into Crime and Delinquency*, 4, 203–11.

Celnick, A. (1985). 'From paradigm to practice in a special probation project', *British Journal of Social Work*, 15 (3), June.

Christie, N. (1977). 'Conflicts as property', *British Journal of Criminology*, 17, 1–15.

Christie, N. (1978). 'Prisons in society, or society as a prison' in J. Freeman (ed.), *Prisons Past and Future*. London, Heinemann.

Christie, N. (1982). *Limits to Pain*. Oxford, Martin Robertson.

Cicourel, A.V. (1964). *Method and Measurement in Sociology*. Glencoe, IL, Free Press.

Cicourel, A.V. (1968). *The Social Organization of Juvenile Justice*. London, Heinemann.

Clarke, J. (1980). 'Social democratic delinquents and Fabian families' in National Deviancy Conference (ed.), *Permissiveness and Control*. London, Macmillan.

Clarke, J. (1985). 'Whose Justice? The Politics of Juvenile Control', *International Journal of the Sociology of Law*, 13, 407–21.

Cohen, S. (1985). *Visions of Social Control*. Cambridge, Polity Press.

Cohen, S.J. (on-going 1985). 'Social enquiry reports: a study of what recommendations are made and what the outcome is in terms of adjudications', Dorset Probation Service.

Collison, M. (1980). 'Questions of juvenile justice' in P. Carlen and M. Collison (eds), *Radical Issues in Criminology*. Oxford, Martin Robertson.

Corrigan, P. (1979). *Schooling the Smash Street Kids*. London, Macmillan.

Cousins, M. and Hussain, A. (1984). *Michel Foucault*. London, Macmillan.

Craib, I. (1984). *Modern Social Theory*. Brighton, Harvester Press.

Davies, M. (1974). 'Social enquiry for the courts', *British Journal of Criminology*, 14 (1), 18–33.

DHSS (1987). *Reports to Courts: Practice Guidelines for Social Workers*. London, HMSO.

Donzelot, J. (1980). *The Policing of Families*. London, Hutchinson.

Douglas, M. (1966). *Purity and Danger*. London, Routledge & Kegan Paul.

Durkheim, E. (1964). *The Division of Labor in Society*. Toronto, Collier-Macmillan.

Eagleton, T. (1976). *Criticism and Ideology*. London, Verso.

Emerson, R. (1969). *Judging Delinquents*. Chicago, Aldine.

Emerson, R.M. (1983). 'Holistic effects in social control decision making', *Law and Society Review*, 17 (3), 425–55.

Estlea, B. (on going 1985). *An Investigation into the Extent of the Unmet Needs of Courts and Clients in Parts of West Sussex*. West Sussex PACS.

Family Policy Studies Centre (1985). *The Family Today: Continuity and Change*, Factsheet 1, September.

Faugeron, C. and Houchon, G. (1987). 'Prison and the penal system: from penology to a sociology of penal policies' *International Journal of the Sociology of Law*, 15, 393–422.

Ford, P. (1972). *Advising Sentencers*. Oxford University Penal Research Unit Occasional Paper No 5. Oxford, Basil Blackwell.

Foucault, M. (1970). *The Order of Things*. London, Tavistock.

Foucault, M. (1974). *The Archaeology of Knowledge*. London, Tavistock.

Foucault, M. (1977). *Discipline and Punish*. Harmondsworth, Penguin.

Foucault, M. (1980). *Power/Knowledge*. Brighton, Harvester Press.

Freeman, M.D.A. (1981). 'The rights of children when they do wrong', *British Journal of Criminology*, 21, 212–26.

Garfinkel, H. (1967). *Studies in Ethnomethodology*. Englewood Cliffs, NJ, Prentice-Hall.

Garland, D. (1981). 'The Birth of the Welfare Sanction', *British Journal of Law and Society*, 8 (1), 29–46.

Garland, D. (1985). *Punishment and Welfare*. Aldershot, Gower.

Garland, D. and Young, P. (eds) (1983). *The Power to Punish: Contemporary Penality and Social Analysis*. London, Heinemann.

Gaskell, E. (1970). *Mary Barton*. Harmondsworth, Penguin.

Giddens, A. (1976). *New Rules of Sociological Method*. London, Hutchinson.

Giddens, A. (1982). *Profiles and Critiques in Social Theory*. London, Macmillan.

Giddens, A. (1984). *The Constitution of Society*. Cambridge, Basil Blackwell.

Goffman, E. (1975). *Frame Analysis: An Essay in the Organization of Experience*. Harmondsworth, Penguin.

Golding, W. (1979). *Pincher Martin*. London, Faber and Faber.

Gombrich, E.H. (1959). *Art and Illusion*. London, Paladin.

Goode, A. (nd). *Observations on SER's After the Act*. Nottinghamshire PACS.

Gouldner, A. (1979). *The Future of the Intellectuals and the Rise of the New Class*. London, Macmillan.

Hall, S. (1979). *Policing the Crisis*. London, Macmillan.

Hall, S. *et al.* (1980). *Culture, Media, Language*. London, Hutchinson.

Hardiker, P. (1975). *Ideologies in Social Enquiry Reports*. Social Science Research Council.

Hardiker, P. (1977). 'Social work ideologies in the probation service', *British Journal of Social Work*, 7 (2), 131–54.

Harris, R. and Webb, D. (1987). *Welfare, Power, and Juvenile Justice*. London, Tavistock.

Harwin, J. (1982). 'The battle for the delinquent' in *The Year Book of Social Policy in Britain 1980–1981*. London, Routledge & Kegan Paul.

Hine, J., McWilliams, W. and Pease, K. (1978). 'Recommendations, Social Information and Sentencing', *Howard Journal*, 17, 91–100.

Hirschi, T. (1969). *Causes of Delinquency*. Los Angeles, University of California Press.

Hogarth, J. (1971). *Sentencing as a Human Process*. Canada, University of Toronto Press.

Holstein, J.A. (1983). 'Grading practices: The construction and use of background knowledge in evaluative decision making', *Human Studies*, 6, 377–92.

Home Office (1983a). 'Social enquiry reports: general guidance on contents', *Home Office Circular No 17*.

Home Office (1983b). 'Social enquiry reports: recommendations relevant to sentencing', *Home Office Circular No. 18*.

Home Office (1986). 'Social enquiry reports', *Home Office Circular No. 92*.

Home Office (1988a). *Criminal Statistics England and Wales 1987*. London, HMSO.

Home Office (1988b). *Criminal Statistics England and Wales Supplementary Tables 1987*, Vol. 5. London, HMSO.

Home Office (1990). *Crime, Justice and Protecting the Public*, Cmnd. 965. London, HMSO.

Horncastle, J.E. (nd). *Making of Probation Orders Without Social Enquiry Reports: An Experiment in the Magistrates' Court.* Bristol Polytechnic Department of Social Studies research project 1983–1985, unpublished.

Horwitz, A. and Wasserman, M. (1980). 'Some misleading conceptions in sentencing research – an example and a reformulation in the juvenile court' *Criminology*, 18 (3), 411–24.

Hudson, B. (1987). *Justice Through Punishment*. London, Macmillan.

Husbands, C.T. (1981). 'The anti-quantitative bias in postwar British sociology' in P. Abrams, *Practice and Progress: British Sociology 1950–1980*. London, Allen & Unwin.

Jones, T. (1986). *The Islington Crime Survey: Crime Victimization and Policing in Inner City London*. Aldershot, Gower.

Joseph, I. and Fritsch, P. (1977). *Disciplines à domicile: l'edification de la famille.* Recherches No. 28, Fonteney-Sous-Bois, Recherches.

Kapardis, A. and Farrington, D. (1981). 'An experimental study of sentencing by magistrates', *Law and Human Behaviour*, 5 (2), 107–21.

Latour, B. (1986). 'The powers of association' in J. Law (ed.), *Power, Action, and Belief: Towards a New Sociology of Knowledge?* Sociological Review Monograph 32, University of Keele/Routledge & Kegan Paul.

Law, J. (1986). 'On power and its tactics: a view from the sociology of science', *Sociological Review*, 34 (1), 1–38.

Law, J. (ed.) (1986). *Power, Action and Belief: Towards a New Sociology of Knowledge?* Sociological Review Monograph 32, University of Keele/Routledge and Kegan Paul.

Lishman, J. (1983). *Research Highlights 5: Social Work with Adult Offenders.* University of Aberdeen, Department of Social Work.

·Lupton, C. and Roberts, G. (1982). *On Record: Young People Appearing Before a Juvenile Court*. Portsmouth, Social Services Research and Intelligence Unit (unpublished).

Macmillan, J. (1975). *Deviant Drivers*. Farnborough, Saxon House.

Macrimmon, K.R. (1976). 'Decision making and problem solving' in M.D. Dunnette (ed.), *Handbook of Industrial and Organizational Psychology*. Chicago, Rand McNally.

March, J.G. and Simon, H.A. (1970). 'Decision making theory' in O. Grusky and G.A. Miller (eds), *The Sociology of Organizations: Basic Studies*. New York, NY, Free Press.

Marsh, C. (1982). *The Survey Method*. London, Allen and Unwin.

Matza, D. (1964). *Delinquency and Drift*. New York, John Wiley.

May, D. (1977). 'Rhetoric and reality: ambiguity in the children's penal system', *British Journal of Criminology*, 17 (3).

May, D. and Smith, G. (1980). 'Gentlemen versus players: lay–professional relations in the administration of juvenile justice', *British Journal of Social Work*, 10, 293–315.

McBarnet, D. (1981). 'Magistrates' courts and the ideology of justice', *British Journal of Law and Society*, 8 (2), 181–97.

McGrew, A.G. and Wilson, M.J. (1974). *Decision Making: Approaches and Analysis*. Manchester, Manchester University Press/Open University.

McWilliams, W.W. (1984). *Variations Among Probation Officers Social Enquiry Reports: Antecedents, Coincidents, and Consequences*. University of Sheffield, PhD thesis.

Millichamp, D., Payne, D. and Howard, T. (1985). 'A matter of natural justice', *Community Care*, 567, June, 25–7.

Morley, D. (1983). 'Cultural transformations: the politics of resistance' in H. Davis and P. Walton, *Language, Image, Media*. Oxford, Basil Blackwell.

Morris, A. *et al.* (1980). *Justice for Children*. London, Macmillan.

Morris, A. and Giller, H. (1983). *Providing Criminal Justice for Children*. London, Edward Arnold.

Morris, A. and Giller, H. (1987). *Understanding Juvenile Justice*. Beckenham, Croom Helm.

Morris, A. and McIsaac, M. (1978). *Juvenile Justice?* London, Heinemann.

Mott, J. (1977). 'Decision making and social enquiry reports in one juvenile court', *British Journal of Social Work*, 7 (4), 421–32.

Muncie, J. (1984). *The Trouble With Kids Today: Youth and Crime in Post-War Britain*. London, Hutchinson.

Murphy, M. and Stanley, S. (nd). *Survey of Social Enquiry Reports*. Inner London PACS.

Neill, A.S. (1970). *Summerhill*. Harmondsworth, Penguin.

O'Byrne, P. (nd). 'Six months probation orders in West Yorkshire', West Yorkshire Probation and After Care Service, research undertaken 1980.

Oppenheim, A. (1976). *Questionnaire Design and Attitude Measurement*. London, Heinemann.

Osborne, S. (1984). 'Social enquiry reports in one juvenile court', *British Journal of Social Work*, 14 (4), 361–78.

Paley, J. and Leeves, R. (1982). 'Some questions about the reverse tariff', *British Journal of Social Work*, 12 (4), 362–80.

Parker, H. (ed.) (1979). *Social Work and the Courts*. London, Edward Arnold.

Parker, H., Casburn, M. and Turnbull, D. (1981). *Receiving Juvenile Justice*. Oxford, Basil Blackwell.

Parker, H. and Giller, H. (1981). 'More and less the same: British delinquency research since the sixties', *British Journal of Criminology*, 21, 230–45.

Parker, H., Sumner, M. and Jarvis, G. (1989). *Unmasking the Magistrates*. Milton Keynes, Open Univesity Press.

Parsloe, P. (1978). *Juvenile Justice in Britain and the United States: The Balance of Needs and Rights*. London, Routledge & Kegan Paul.

Pearson, G. (1985). 'Lawlessness, modernity, and social change: a historical appraisal', *Theory, Culture and Society*, 2 (3), 15–35.

Pearson, R. (1980). 'Popular justice and the lay magistracy: the two faces of lay participation' in Z. Bankowski and G. Mungham, *Essays in Law and Society*. London, Routledge & Kegan Paul.

Pengelly, H. (1985). *Juvenile Justice Under the Tories: The Example of Oxford*. Norwich, University of East Anglia/Social Work Today Social Work Monograph No. 34.

Perry, F.G. (1974). *Information for the Court*. London, Institute of Criminology.

Phillips, D. (1973). *Abandoning Method*. London, Jossey-Bass.

Pitts, J. (1988). *The Politics of Juvenile Crime*. London, Sage.

Pratt, J. (1983). 'Reflections on the approach of 1984: recent developments in social control in the UK' *International Journal of the Sociology of Law*, 11, November, 358–60.

Pratt, J. (1985). 'Juvenile justice, social work, and social control: the need for positive thinking', *British Journal of Social Work*, 15, 1–24.

Reynolds, F. (1982). 'Social work influence on juvenile court disposals', *British Journal of Social Work*, 12 (1), 65–76.

Roberts, J. and Roberts, C. (1982). 'Social enquiry reports and sentencing', *The Howard Journal*, 21, 76–93.

Salaman, G. (1980). 'Organizations as constructors of reality' in G. Salaman and K. Thompson, *Control and Ideology in Organizations*. Milton Keynes, Open University Press.

Schutz, A. (1972). *The Phenomenology of the Social World*. London, Heinemann.

Schutz, A. and Luckmann, T. (1974). *The Structures of the Life World*. London, Heinemann.

Smith, G. and May, D. (1980). 'Executing "decisions" in children's hearings', *Sociology*, 14, 591–601.

Stafford, E. and Hill, J. (1987). 'The tariff, social inquiry reports and the sentencing of juveniles', *British Journal of Criminology*, 27 (4), 411–20.

Streatfeild (1961). *Report of the Interdepartmental Committee on the Business of the Criminal Courts*, Cmnd. 1289. London, HMSO.

Sumner, M., Jarvis, G. and Parker, H. (1988). 'Objective or objectionable? School reports in the juvenile court', *Youth and Policy*, 23.

Swift, D., Winn, V. and Bramer, D. (1979). 'A sociological approach to the design of information systems', *Journal of the American Society for Information Science*, July, 215–23.

Thorpe, J. (1979). 'Social enquiry reports: a survey', *Home Office Research Study No. 48*.

Thorpe, J. and Pease, K. (1976). 'The relationship between recommendations made to the court and sentences passed', *British Journal of Criminology*, 16, 393–94.

Turner, R. (ed.) (1974). *Ethnomethodology*. Harmondsworth, Penguin.

Tutt, N. and Giller, H. (1984). *Social Inquiry Reports*. Lancaster Social Information Systems. (Audio tape.)

Webb, D. and Hardiker, P. (1983). 'Some answers about the reverse tariff: a reply to Paley and Leeves', *British Journal of Social Work*, 13 (2), 207–18.

Weizenbaum, J. (1984). *Computer Power and Human Reason*. Harmondsworth, Pelican.

White, S. (1972). 'The effect of social enquiry reports on sentencing decisions', *British Journal of Criminology*, 12 (3).

Whitehead, P. and Macmillan, J. (1985). 'Checks or blank cheque?', *Probation Journal*, 32 (3), September, 87–9.

Williamson, H. (1980). 'Defence and Mitigation in the Juvenile Court: the role of the solicitor in juvenile justice' in Z. Bankowski and G. Mungham (eds), *Essays in Law and Society*. London, Routledge & Kegan Paul.

Willis, P. (1977). *Learning to Labour*. Farnborough, Saxon House.

Wilson, T.D. and Streatfeild, D.R. (1977). 'Information needs in local authority social services departments: an interim report on project INISS', *Journal of Documentation*, 33 (4), 277–93.

Worsley, H. (1849). *Juvenile Depravity*. London, Gilpin. Cited in A. Morris and H. Giller (1987), *Understanding Juvenile Justice*, Beckenham, Croom Helm.

Young, M. and Whitty, G. (1977). *Society, State and Schooling*. Ringmer, Falmer Press.

Index